THE MAGNIFICENT MISTAKE

How you can earn more from failure
than you learn from success

Ion Valis

Pop Philosophy Press
Montreal

Published by Pop Philosophy Press.

Library of Congress Cataloguing-in-Publication Data
Valis, Ion
1. Leadership 2. Management. 3. Magnificent Mistakes.
ISBN: 0993931502
ISBN 9780993931505

First Edition

MOM: I WISH THAT YOU WERE HERE TO SEE THIS HAPPEN, BUT I KNOW YOU'RE LOOKING DOWN FROM ABOVE — AND SMILING.

CONTENTS

PART I: LAYING THE FOUNDATION

WHY: 3

CHAPTER 1 - THE MISUNDERSTOOD MISTAKE
| WHY YOU EARN MORE FROM FAILURE THAN YOU LEARN
FROM SUCCESS 3

Erik Weihenmayer and learning how to see with your tongue |
Success sells; but what does it tell? | Focusing on failure instead
of studying success | When the light (bulb) came on | Failure
is essential to success | Winning by losing | Don't just limit your
mistakes — profit from them | Cracking the Talent Code

| 8) **Put out a Quarterly Failure Report and Keep a Mistake Journal** | 9) **Have a To Not Do List alongside your To Do List** | 10) **Make MMs part of your team's KPIs** | 11) **Don't treat all errors equally** | 12) **Hire with failure in mind**: look for people who have failed twice over those who have succeeded once

AUTHOR'S NOTE

WHY YOU SHOULD READ *THE MAGNIFICENT MISTAKE*

This is a book for you, your boss or (if you're the boss) your employees, as well as for your partner, spouse, friend, sibling, son or daughter.

It's for entrepreneurs and executives, leaders and followers, coaches and team players. For grizzled veterans of the workplace wars and for dewy-eyed newcomers just starting out. It's for volunteers and not-for-profit workers as well as aspiring billionaires. In short, it's for anyone who makes mistakes — small ones, big ones, personal ones, professional ones but especially the same ones over and over. However, it's less focused on why we commit errors, and more on what to do after making one. It provides a key to unlocking the past, so you can also unlock your future.

The lessons will have specific relevance to certain people, including Business executives and other professionals who will find the material useful for improving themselves and their processes.

Most successful people are good at identifying early their strengths and weaknesses. As we progress in our careers, we rely on our assets to take us forward, but we must also assess and identify our liabilities to keep them from holding us back. It is in plumbing our mistakes that we come face to face with those chinks in our professional armor; and only then do we gain the insight to address those weaknesses by managing around them. The book will provide professionals with a framework to systematically learn from their mistakes.

It's not enough, however, to conscientiously address your own flaws. These days, it may be necessary for a manager to correct his team or even his entire company's mistakes. After all, one of a leader's principal responsibilities is to ensure the organization's strategy and overall direction is sound. Just as a captain sets a ship's destination but also takes action when it veers off course, so must today's executives make constant course corrections for their enterprises to successfully navigate today's challenging business climate. *The Magnificent Mistake* will provide these leaders with sophisticated but practical tools to help them 'master' their team's miscues.

The final way in which these concepts can enhance professional fortunes is by enabling you to learn from your competitor's mistakes. More often than not, business is a zero-sum game. If you win, your competition loses; conversely, if they win, you lose. One doesn't have to be Sun Tzu to understand the strategic value in seizing advantage from the errors of your rivals. This can be accomplished either by learning to avoid their fate, or by transforming their experiences into your own research and development. After all, the business concept of second-mover advantage — the idea there is a benefit in launching a product second, not first — is predicated on this type of thinking. In both cases, being able to learn from your competition's mistakes can lead to a significant competitive advantage, and I will outline a process to do just that.

What if you're not a captain of industry, or if you simply run a company of one (You, Inc.)?

Moreover, what if your notion of 'competitive advantage' is limited to your Saturday tennis matches or even more personal battles?

You don't need to be responsible for the performance of a team or the fate of a company to benefit from learning how to make the most of your mistakes. After all, the daily errors we make can serve a purpose if we become skilled at distilling why they happened and determine how to avoid committing them again. Some of these fumbles are frivolous, such as always forgetting where we put our keys, while others are so crucial they can sometimes sabotage couples and careers. At both ends of this spectrum, however, errors are annoying, especially if we realize they are largely preventable. Why go a minute more without mining them for lessons? Why not take a moment or two to learn some key skills that promise significant personal development and improved performance as well? The tools you will discover are not a set of abstractions, but rather advice that you can use right away, every day.

They say that the only certainties in life are death and taxes. I would add a third: mistakes. We are condemned to constantly commit errors; perfection is neither desirable nor, frankly, possible. Contrary to what you might suspect, I firmly believe we must have the freedom to fail in order to succeed.

Errors are useful — as learning opportunities as well as sources of personal and professional development and significant competitive advantage. They are useless when they reoccur, and when they systematically sabotage your happiness or your career.

If you make mistakes (and we all do), this book is for you.

It doesn't matter if your errors simply impact your golf game or seriously imperil your company's good name; either way, you will benefit from learning how to leverage them. You owe it to yourself to interrupt the cycle that sets you up to fail again and again.

This book will provide a blueprint for bringing out your best by learning how to weed out the worst. Over the next pages, we'll draw on the diverse fields of psychology, business, military operations and medicine to identify 'best practices' for dealing with mistakes. We'll look at outstanding performances, from the record-breaking gold medal run of Michael Phelps to the rise of Amazon, to understand precisely how great successes are forged from earlier failures. By examining how autopsies are conducted to the way the U.S. military performs after-action reviews following missions, we'll identify specific forensic skills you'll need to break down and analyze mistakes in a systematic, structured way. These tools, we will also see, can be applied in almost any context.

While most people accept they should learn from errors, few do so as a matter of course. Fewer still do it in a conscious, habitual and strategic manner. In these pages, I approach the problem of mistake management in an intellectually rigorous yet real world tested framework. By combining original thinking with current examples and cross-disciplinary best practices, this book is a guidebook to transforming your errors into magnificent mistakes.[1] It will show you how to stop chronic errors, improve your performance as an individual or an organization, and help you become a better decision-maker. In the process, it will also change your attitude towards failure.

PREFACE

THE ORIGIN OF THE IDEA

Surprisingly, I remember the moment like it was yesterday. It was September 1998, I was sitting in my first strategy class at London Business School, and we were talking about Southwest Airlines. In most business schools, much of the learning comes from examining a detailed analysis of a company's experience — a case study — overcoming a specific challenge, and discussing the key lessons. Often, these exercises are insightful, if not fascinating, and this one delivered the goods.

If you've ever flown on Southwest, you'd be interested to know why they're one of the world's most successful airlines. For one, they went completely against the grain of the industry at the time and rejected the familiar "hub-and-spoke" model of flight routing (where to get from Charlotte to Calgary you'd have to fly through a hub airport like Chicago) for a point-to-point (San Diego to Las Vegas) system. Second, they strove to have only one type of airplane in their fleet (the Boeing 737). This represented a strategic masterstroke, because it allowed them to train their mechanics to repair a single model of aircraft using one the same set of parts. Because every plane in the fleet was the same, they could develop and then transfer loading and unloading best practices to all crews, thus shaving crucial minutes of downtime on each flight (and ensuring on-time departure). Southwest went further, studying Formula One racing car crew pits to see how they became so fast at refitting their vehicles in seconds while in the "pits".

They also plowed their profits into buying the newest models thereby keeping their fleet maintenance costs the lowest in the industry. Finally, they hired up-beat, energetic people as their flight crew, and instructed them to have fun while prioritizing customer service above all.[1]

As I sat there transfixed by the brilliance of Southwest's strategy, I had a little epiphany. This is a great blueprint to launch a low-cost, point-to-point airline; too bad Southwest beat me to it!

I realized at that moment that while it was enlightening to understand why Southwest had been so successful in launching their airline in 1967, these insights had little prescriptive value to me today. I then started noticing almost all of the case studies we studied while getting our MBAs, and the articles we read about in business journals later, as managers post-MBA, were *success* stories. For every occasional disappointment we examined, there were ten triumphs trumpeted. It prompted me to wonder how useful it actually was to study success, when setbacks might offer more lasting lessons. I didn't realize it at the time, but so began my path towards looking more closely at mistakes, and stress-testing the idea their examination might prove to be more fruitful for employees and executives alike.

What I discovered is this: success strategies are often nontransitive. That's a fancy way of saying it's very difficult to apply them to another situation and expect a similar result. It's a flawed presumption what worked for another person or organization will work for you and yours. There is rarely a specific recipe for success — at least not one you can easily reverse-engineer, or copy from someone else's victories and then repeat. Ironically, I came to believe the only true formula for making failure less likely is to consistently learn from your mistakes.

Correcting errors, and figuring out how to avoid them in the first place, is crucial to improving performance. This is true whether you are an Olympic swimmer striving for immortality, a young professional looking for a promotion or simply a person looking to get better at whatever you do.

I've spent the last five years thinking on and exploring this idea in depth. I combined this curiosity with twenty-three years of professional experience — of mistakes made and wisdom gained in both the public and private sectors, as an employee and as an executive, in North America as well as working abroad — to examine how we can make every error a teachable moment. I first looked at how great companies address setbacks, and whether there was a correlation between their treatment of past failures and a track record of subsequent successes. I also analyzed exceptional performers, from the worlds of sport, politics, war and even the arts, to see if this pattern on turning errors into excellence held true in many walks of life. I then distilled the lessons learned from all of these case studies into a conceptual framework and a practical checklist to enable individuals and organizations alike to quickly and systematically learn from their mistakes. Finally, I tested the idea in the real world — first in my life, but then through the experiences of the individuals and organizations to which I provide consulting and strategic advice.

Those years of research, reflection and evaluation yielded some key insights, and they can be summed up in these simple but powerful ideas:

Learning from mistakes is a superb strategy for success in your personal and professional life. It is the most direct,

most powerful yet least practiced way to improve yourself or
your company's performance. Finally, one of the best-kept
secrets of truly successful people and organizations is they
habitually and systematically profit from their errors and
those of their competitors.

Why is this so important? For a variety of reasons, we have
lost sight of the pedagogical power of errors. However, sometimes the simplest ideas often have the most impact.

It has become trendy to focus exclusively on the importance of developing people's assets instead of correcting their
faults. I accept the intrinsic appeal of this approach. As Tim
Ferriss, author of the *Four Hour Work Week* notes, "it is far
more lucrative and fun to leverage your strengths instead of
attempting to fix all of the chinks in your armor."[2]

It is hard work to face, let alone fix, the errors we make
along the way. But we cannot succeed on our strengths alone.
Triumph is too temporary, and failure is too frequent, for us
to limit ourselves to working with only half of the tools at our
disposal. Business leaders like Amazon's Jeff Bezos stress the
importance of playing to our strengths but also actively managing around our weaknesses. Peerless performers — such as
the crack U.S. Army special operators known colloquially as
Delta Force — are always working on their shortcomings to
improve their mission-readiness. Later on in the book, we examine both to understand why.

While it may be more fun to emphasize your strengths, it
is actually *easier* to improve your performance by addressing
your flaws. After all, we can control our mistakes but little
else in life. People are often their own worst enemies precisely because they first ignore, and then keep committing, the
same miscues time and time again. But mistakes are often

the difference between winning and losing; in life, we need to limit unforced errors as much as we leverage our biggest assets.

As is often the case, the truth lies somewhere in between these two approaches. Deciding between building strengths and correcting flaws is, in fact, a false choice. We should do both. But that's not what our society teaches us to do. Errors are ignored at best and covered up at worst. It's a mistake to discount the value of mistakes, however. In fact, as I will argue, I believe we have far more to earn from failure than we can learn from success.

The challenge, however, lies in how to act on this paradox. Eleanor Roosevelt provided us with a little inspiration when she counseled to "learn from the mistakes of others. You can't live long enough to make them all yourself." Playwright William Saroyan added some philosophical guidance when he wrote: "good people are good because they've come to wisdom through failure." Taken together, these two epigrams suggest what we call 'wisdom' can be described simply as learning from your mistakes and from those of others.

The following pages will explore the many ways in which one can do just that. In the process, I will propose a way to systematically examine our errors.

On one level, this is common sense; however, that doesn't mean it's common practice. The reality is individuals and organizations rarely leverage their miscues, let alone in a reflexive manner. How is it, for example, that large financial institutions maintain risk management functions but not mistake management ones, particularly since risk is a relative uncertainty (by definition), while missteps are much more likely to occur? And why do individuals consistently refuse to face their mistakes, thereby running the risk of repeating them?

In practice, it does not make sense. In my view, errors are a bit like imperfections one can correct: would you continue with blurry vision if you knew that glasses or contact lenses could give you perfect eyesight? Of course not. But this is what people and organizations do whenever they fail to look critically at why they failed.

Not only is this approach nonsensical, it's also a-historical. Whether we choose to confront them or not, mistakes represent a piece of our past. Learning from errors (ours and others) is part and parcel of learning from history. As Spanish philosopher George Santayana said: "those who cannot remember the past, are condemned to repeat it." What's more, many mistakes, and all second errors, are preventable because they are triggered by common, modifiable behaviors.

For all these reasons, leveraging past mistakes is fundamental to future achievement. On an individual level, seizing the lessons from one's stumbles can lead to what I call second-act successes. In a more competitive environment, an opponent's blunders can provide a valuable blueprint of pitfalls to sidestep. In both cases, setbacks become tremendous sources of strategic insight. Taken together, these conclusions reveal the central paradox behind the *Magnificent Mistake* concept: studying setbacks — yours and your competitors — is your first step to success.

In 1965, Peter Drucker, the inventor of modern management theory, published a slim volume that came to revolutionize the way people manage themselves. The book, *The Effective Executive,* remains one of the best-selling business titles of all time, and it is required reading even today.[3]

My goal is to be inspired by his example and transform the way people look at mistakes. I believe everyone can benefit from this change in mindset. One of the few things we all share is a propensity for committing errors. We also have a common tendency to avoid confronting our missteps, let alone mining them for the lessons they hold. As we will learn, mistakes can become teaching moments — but only if we have the courage, commitment and capability to make the most of them.

꩜

INTRODUCTION

THE DIFFERENCE BETWEEN GOLD AND SILVER

Beijing, August 16, 2008. As the eight swimmers hit the wall almost in unison, the crowd in the Water Cube leaped to their feet and strained to see who was ahead. With only fifty meters to go, Michael Phelps took the turn way back in seventh place. It was the Men's Final of the 100 meter butterfly, which meant the distance separating first and last was measured in hundredths of a second — sixty-two, to be exact. Still, Phelps' historic bid for a seventh goal medal was in jeopardy if he couldn't find the trademark afterburners that made him such a prolific finisher in the pool. His Beijing odyssey of seventeen races across eight events was perilously close to coming to an end. Serbian sprinter Milorad Cavic was seconds from becoming the man who denied Michael Phelps his quest to achieve Olympic immortality.

With thirty-five meters left, Cavic closed in on the finish line clearly in the lead. Phelps labored to catch up, propelling his arms in a wide, rhythmic arc. Those arms are one of the keys to Michael Phelps' swimming success. In fact, he has a body almost genetically engineered for aqua dynamics. He's tall, but at six-foot-four Phelps is not much taller than your average college swimmer. However, his disproportionately long wingspan of six feet, seven inches (most people have arm spans equal to their height) give him the length of a taller man and the propulsive power of canoe paddles attached to each shoulder. Add to that his relatively short legs, thin torso, famously flipper-size feet (he wears size 14) and hyper-flexible ankles, and you have all the genetic ingredients of a swimming machine.

Despite these natural advantages, though, Phelps was still trailing Cavic with only a few body lengths to go. The din of the crowd became deafening as those final, almost impossibly tense moments played out. The two competitors in lanes four and five were so close only the TV audience watching at home, aided by the broadcast network's computer imagery and sensors, could tell who was in the lead.

As the two swimmers began their final stroke to the wall, Phelps stared down into the depths of the pool, at the black line marking his way, but perhaps at the end of his dreams as well. He had been at this since he was eleven years old, and had trained every day — Christmas, New Year, his birthday — for five straight years, logging hundreds of thousands of lonely, determined hours in the hopes of harnessing his athletic potential but also of making history. Peak performance specialists have written about how it takes at least 10,000 hours of 'deliberate practice' to become expert at something, and Phelps had certainly put in that time and more. His swimming coach Bob Bowman had devised now-legendary training regimens for his prodigy, including a torturous 10,000-meter workout for time. Translating the swimming jargon, this meant Phelps raced for 10,000 meters (ten kilometers) as fast as he could for two and a half hours — for *practice*.[1]

But on August 16, 2008, all those years spent, sacrificed, some might say, in the pool in the pursuit of that goal were coming down to a few short seconds. Phelps could now only rely on his muscle memory. His training told him to stay focused until the last millisecond. He propelled his body forward with one final stretch of the arms and kept his head down to maintain proper racing streamline. Cavic, on the other hand, lifted his head ever so slightly just before touching the mark, creating a minuscule amount of drag that slowed his body precisely 1/100 of a second. Both men touched the wall in a splash of white water, seemingly at the same exact time.

It was literally a photo finish. For a second, not the swimmers, or the audience, or the announcers on TV knew who'd won. Both Cavic and Phelps turned to the scoreboard to see the result. Asked about that last stroke later, Phelps admitted he was sure he had misjudged the finish and had lost the race in that moment. But as Phelps looked up, the screen flashed his Olympic-record time of 50.58 seconds, exactly 1/100 of a second faster than Milorad Cavic.

It was Cavic's tiny but untimely tilt of the head upwards that had given Michael Phelps the race, his seventh goal medal and a shot at athletic eternity. Phelps went on to win his final event and secured his place in Olympic lore, while Cavic is now destined to become an answer to a *Trivial Pursuit* question.

The difference between gold and silver, between history and trivia, between success and failure often comes down to a minute yet monumental mistake.

In the case of Milorad Cavic vs. Michael Phelps in Beijing that day, it was an almost incomprehensible 1/100 of a second. As *Sports Illustrated* asked after the historic race, "What is one-hundredth of a second? It is thirty times faster than the blink of an eye. It is 1/36 of the time it takes a 100-mph fastball to reach the plate. It is the blur of lightning striking. It is a flutter of time so minuscule the mind cannot comprehend it, and yet that is what Milorad Cavic has left to comprehend."[2]

Until that fateful moment, Cavic had done what was considered improbable if not impossible — to race faster than a man almost genetically ordained and painstakingly trained to become the world's greatest swimmer. But the ultimate source of Cavic's undoing was not his opponent's extraordinary athletic gifts or years of practice honing them, but rather Michael Phelps' ability, at the most crucial moment of the most important race in his life, to avoid a critical miscue.

Cavic would have beaten history's greatest Olympian had he not committed that final error, and his crushing defeat teaches us a vital lesson: mistakes *matter*.

Would it surprise you to learn that Michael Phelps spent countless hours in the pool preparing for unexpected challenges, and more importantly how to deal with them? For example, Coach Bowman would regularly have him swim lengths with his eyes bandaged so, if his goggles filled up with water, as they did during one of the Beijing races, Phelps could operate 'blind' on a stroke count alone. Phelps developed 'muscle memory' for almost every contingency, which meant when a crucial moment in the race came his body knew what to do. His training is what saved him in Beijing that day. It was from having made every mistake in practice — and learning how to avoid them in the races — that Michael Phelps won the race, the gold medal, and the place in history he now occupies. *(Later in the book, we will revisit America's greatest Olympian after the 2012 London Games to see if he remains magnificent. Stay tuned.)*

As the example above shows us, the difference between victory and defeat can, indeed, come turn on a tiny yet crucial error. This book will show you ways to leverage your current and future mistakes. In doing, so, it will set you on your path towards earning more from failure than you are learning from success.

THE ROAD MAP

This book focuses on the why, who and the how of that simple premise. It then closes with the answer to the question: what now?

Chapter 1: Why

In Part One, I lay out the arguments for a broad rethinking of mistakes as we know them. We start from the assumption we've been wrong all along in how we view errors and introduce the idea of the misunderstood mistake. Instead of denying missteps, we need to redefine our view of them. There are, in fact, real and significant benefits to failing, and this section will explore them all.

Almost everyone agrees it's a good idea to learn from errors. Who wouldn't? But few have explored why it's so critical to do so. I will make the definitive case.

Chapter 2: Who

Next, we will look at some top-performing organizations that make a special effort to tackle their mistakes. We will discover how some of the world's best companies, from Amazon to Toyota, as well as two of the world's most effective military organizations — the U.S. Army and the Israeli Air Force — systematically address errors in order to identify 'best practices' that can be applied beyond these areas.

All winners learn from their missteps. I've studied hundreds of great achievers, teams and organizations, and I can tell you they all share one common trait: they have the discipline to learn from mistakes (theirs, and their competitors). Above all, successful people fail. But success rarely happens on the first try, so it's vital to capitalize on those early attempts by learning from them.

Chapter 3: How

How we can best do that is the subject of the second part of the book, where I give you a process and a toolbox for you to master your mistakes. Both are critical because understanding we need to learn from our errors is not enough; we need to know how.

This section will present the definitive blueprint for how to make the most of your mistakes: the Magnificent Mistake Checklist™. It is a six-step process captured in the acronym M.A.S.T.E.R.™ I will also introduce a number of new tools ands concepts I've developed to support this framework, including Mistake Maps, Traps and Journals as well as the Error Gene™.

Chapter 4: Now

The closing chapter focuses on how the checklist and tools can be applied in the real world. I conclude by describing the 12 Magnificent Mistake Habits™ you should implement in your life, team or organization.

There is one final point: this is an optimistic book. It is <u>not</u> about wrapping yourself around the axle of your previous mistakes; rather, it's about liberating yourself from them — from the monotony of repeating them to the tyranny of their consequences. In the southern United States, they have a saying: "there is no education in the second kick of a mule."[3] I hope this book helps you to consistently avoid getting that second kick.

Before we can accomplish the end goal, however, we need to start with the first principles. Let's begin by looking more closely at why miscues are so misunderstood in the first place.

PART I: LAYING THE FOUNDATION

1

WHY:

THE MISUNDERSTOOD MISTAKE | WHY YOU EARN MORE FROM FAILURE THAN YOU LEARN FROM SUCCESS

"Experience is the name we give to our mistakes." **Oscar Wilde**

Imagine standing on the tallest point on the planet, a summit so high you can see the curvature of the Earth. Picture yourself being buffeted by winds generated by the jet stream (yes, *that* jet stream) because the sliver of rock on which you're perched reaches over 29,000 feet above sea level, where only airplanes usually tread. Then try to conceive of tackling such a challenge — conquering Mount Everest – despite being completely blind.

Only one person would dare such a feat, and that is Erik Wiehenmayer. Erik is not your typical mountain climber or, for that matter, your typical man. Blinded at the age of 13, he captained his high school wrestling team, graduated from university, earned a master's degree, and then proceeded to scale the highest peaks in America and Africa, ride a bicycle across Vietnam, run marathons and in 2001 became the first and only blind person to climb the world's tallest summit. He has since gone on the complete the Seven Summits, getting to the top of the highest peaks on each continent.

How, you may ask, can a blind man climb mountains? Believe it or not, Erik did so by learning to 'see' with his tongue. Since 2003, Erik has used a machine that translates distance, shape and size data into electric impulses he 'reads' with his mouth (though he did not use the device in the historic 2001 ascent of Everest). Called a Brain Port, it overlays a grid of electrodes over his tongue and tells his mind what we normally 'see' with our eyes.[1]

Neuroscientist and author David Eagleman tells the story of the blind climber in his superb book on the secret lives of the brain, Incognito. As he points out, "if it seems strange that nerve signals … can represent vision, bear in mind that your own sense of vision is carried by nothing but millions of nerve signals … To the brain, it doesn't matter where those pulses come from — the eyes, the ears, or something else entirely. As long as they consistently correlate with your own movements as you push, thump and kick things, your brain can construct the direct perception we call vision."

Magnificent Mistakes | George Mallory's 3 failed attempts to summit Everest

Description: *George Mallory made three unsuccessful attempts at being the first person to summit Mount Everest in the 1920s. He died on his third try in May 1924.[2]*

What Went Wrong? *When George Mallory and his climbing partner Sandy Irvine were last seen it was presumed they died a scant 800 vertical feet below the top of Everest. Since the discovery of Mallory's body (75 years later in May, 1999) on the mountain, a debate has raged about whether or not Mallory reached the summit before dying.*

Lesson Learned: *While Mallory failed in his bids (and paid the ultimate price, with his life), historian Wade Davis has called those efforts "heroic failures" because they paved the way for Edmund Hillary and Tenzing Norgay to reach the summit in 1953. Mallory's pioneering route up the mountain, including the stationing of camps along the way, blazed a trail Hillary would ultimately follow to the top of the world.* **Sometimes, events appear as failures at first but may become something else in hindsight.**

Eagleman concludes that Erik Weihenmayer's exploits "remind us that we see not with our eyes but rather with our brains."[3]

This is a critical observation, relevant to the act of 'seeing' but also about how we perceive obstacles and events. Contrary to popular belief, vision is not an objective reality so much as it is a language that we must master. Indeed, people who recover their sight after years of blindness don't immediately see the world clearly; they must actually learn to see again.

If a blind man can be taught to see with his tongue, can we come to see things differently when we look at mistakes? This chapter is all about the path we need to take to retrain our brains and interpret errors in a new light.

Mistakes have been misunderstood throughout history. We have been wrong all along in the way we look at miscues. Rather than denying or stigmatizing them, we need to redefine our view of them. In fact, the seeds of a future success lie within each error we make. There are real and significant benefits to failure, as we shall now explore.

It's hard to fault people for acting like their errors might end up on their epitaph. Facing mistakes is not fun. We're forced to acknowledge we're not perfect, and that what happened was our fault. The desire to suppress such thoughts is hardwired in human nature. We find it difficult to accept responsibility on our own terms, let alone admit blunders publicly.

It's no wonder people gravitate more towards triumphant stories. Inspiration is far more uplifting than contrition. We need to resist the siren song of success however, and focus instead on a strategy built on the small wins afforded indirectly by miscues. Failure doesn't so much teach you the lessons you want as the ones that you need.

I want to help rehabilitate the misunderstood mistake. We should return to an era when errors were considered steppingstones to a greater truth, a time when Irish author James Joyce's famous observation "mistakes are the portals of discovery" summed up the prevailing view on setbacks.

In a different, less superficial time, poets, playwrights and philosophers sung the praises of mistakes. It is only recently we have come to lionize success and stigmatize failure so starkly. In fact, there is a long tradition of viewing blunders in a largely positive light. Alexander Pope offered: "a man should never be ashamed to own he has been in the wrong, which is but saying... that he is wiser today than he was yesterday." George Bernard Shaw was of the same opinion, pointing out "a life spent making mistakes is not only more honorable but more useful than a life spent doing nothing." The French philosopher Michel de Montaigne also suggested we think differently about it as well, pointing out "there are defeats more triumphant than victories."

In our rush to embrace modernity, we seem to have forgotten the wisdom of the ancients. They understood there are virtues to failure. We need to rediscover that truth, and redefine our whole approach towards mistakes. But first, we must overcome our obsession with success.

SUCCESS SELLS; BUT WHAT DOES IT TELL?

Visit any bookstore in America and you will be amazed at how the business section, in particular, is filled with books on success. The sheer number of books chronicling the virtues of achievement is astounding — more than 191,000 titles came up in a recent search on "success" on Amazon — until one realizes how many of them are consistently on the top seller lists as well. Magazine racks trumpet much the same message, as titles from *Fortune* to *Success* offer homage to this culture while others, such as *The Robb Report*, are content to simply allude to it. There is even a line of office decoration products, aptly named 'Successories', that seeks to: "set the tone for success" (their words) by combining gauzy images and motivational quotations from inspirational people.

We appear to have an insatiable appetite for such stories, in order to better understand and presumably emulate them. The only problem with that approach is … it's wrong.

One of the best-kept secrets about success is that it often comes as a surprise. Sure, we always read about people who were 'destined for greatness' by dint of being child prodigies in their fields. We somehow always knew that Mark Zuckerberg would eventually become one of the world's most successful CEOs, or that LeBron James would live up to his promise and emerge as the dominant basketball player of his era. Their triumphs were expected, some might say ordained by their exceptional gifts demonstrated early in life. But would we say the same about Russell Crowe, Russell Wilson or even Russell Brand? When Crowe started as a wannabe rock star (under the pseudonym 'Russ Le Roq') or starring in the Australian soap opera *Neighbours*, did anybody really expect that he'd go on to become one of the most bankable movie stars of his generation? When Wilson played three mostly unremarkable seasons as the starting quarterback at North Carolina State University before transferring to Wisconsin for his final season, then was drafted with the 75th pick overall, did Seattle Seahawks fans feel confident that he would lead them to a Super Bowl victory a mere two years later? Finally, when Russell Simmons started a little music label called Def Jam in 1983, no one could have predicted he would ride the emerging hip hop music wave to unprecedented success, and in the process turn himself into a business magnate with a reported net worth of over 340 million dollars.

Success **surprises**. Those who we expect will be outstanding — think class valedictorians and prom queens — don't always end up so, while many who seemed undistinguished at first blush go on to have enormously accomplished careers. It's not just a question of the tortoise eventually outpacing the hare. Despite our seemingly deep understanding of how the world works, we still don't really know what leads to success let alone how to predict it. This is why we are so often caught off-guard by its emergence in places we never thought possible. For every aptitude test we devise and formula for winning we improvise, success remains an elusive outcome to forecast.

What's more, it is often **serendipitous**. Opportunity occurs, to paraphrase Seneca, when luck meets preparation. Ask almost any successful person and they will admit — if they're honest — good fortune played as much a role in their accomplishments as their abilities. Would any of us know the name of Sarah Palin if the once obscure governor of a faraway state had not been the winsome winner of the 2008 Republican US vice-presidential sweepstakes? How much of Kim Kardashian's emergence as a reality TV sensation is owed to simple chance and being in the right place at the right time? All I'm suggesting is success in these instances would not have been possible without a lot of luck.

Another characteristic of success is that it is also often **spontaneous**. Good things sometimes just happen, without the benefit of a specific trigger. When rock bands finally break through with their first chart topping single, can they ever point to what they did differently *this time* versus the previous five albums they put out? When a writer like George RR Martin is 'discovered' with his breakthrough novel *A Game of Thrones*, can he fully explain why that page-turner was made into an HBO series in 2011 when it initially did not garner any attention upon publication in 1996? It's not that these artists suddenly became talented, or finally discovered what they were doing wrong all along. Triumphs often occur after many years of disappointment, without rhyme, reason or rational explanation.

Success is also often **the sum of small steps**, as opposed to the result of some single, seismic event. Most people believe the Beatles became an overnight sensation when they famously appeared on *The Ed Sullivan Show* in February 1964. But as Malcolm Gladwell points out his book *Outliers*, the Liverpudlian quartet had, in fact, been perfecting their craft by playing literally hundreds of gigs in Hamburg, Germany from 1960 to 1962.[4] Michael Phelps did not actually burst onto the scene in Beijing, since he'd won six gold medals in the Athens Olympics four years earlier. Rather, his success was a direct result of the decade of training he put in from ages eleven to twenty-one in the run-up to the 2008 Olympics and his date with destiny. We may learn about an athlete or artist in some sudden and spectacular circumstances, but their achievements are almost certainly the culmination of their slow, steady, methodical commitment to excellence.

There is an interesting paradox about achievement that follows from what we've just discovered. While big wins often come after a series of many little ones along the way, success also tends to manifest itself as a **solitary** and often **short-lived** event. Lightning does indeed strike, but it rarely does twice. The term 'one-hit wonders' came about for this very reason; even a rock band with a blockbuster single can only move from 'sensation' to 'success' when it follows up the first hit with a second and a third. This is why we still listen today to Depeche Mode (well, some of us do anyway) but are mercifully spared any more Kajagoogoo albums, and why Lee Child's novels still sell but Milan Kundera's works after *The Unbearable Lightness of Being* sadly do not.

Triumphs are transient. Just ask lottery winners, who despite their huge windfalls return to their pre-jackpot levels of general happiness within a year of claiming their prizes. Or talk to the CEOs of the companies who were profiled in the seminal 1982 business book *In Search of Excellence* by Tom Peters and Robert Waterman, as half of their enterprises were no longer in business a mere ten years later.[5] Success doesn't usually overstay its welcome.

Finally, I should point out success is **rare.** At least it should be; if it were more commonplace, would we regard it the same way? In fact, our view of victory is informed by its perceived infrequency. If more than one team won the Super Bowl every year, fans would find another way to single out a championship season. If all books were considered best sellers, then we'd have to invent another accolade to differentiate them. Our society defines success because of its singularity, not in spite of it. Its very uncommonness makes it both valued as a result and yet valueless as a road map.

This philosophical survey has a purpose: to demonstrate triumphs may not be the worthwhile subjects of examination they initially seem. First, they are surprising, serendipitous and spontaneous. Second, they are also the sum of steps rather than the result of one single event. Finally, they are short-lived. All of this leads to a provocative thought: have we been largely wasting our time studying successes all this time?

There is no magic formula for winning, at least not one that can be reproduced. You can't often get the same results simply by reverse engineering or replicating other people's triumphs. We have been sold on continuously studying success despite the fact it teaches us little of real value. These stories are popular because of the mistaken belief that somewhere therein lays the secret to your own future victories.

Our society has a tendency to glorify winners while heaping scorn on losers. But we've been wrong all along. We need to rethink how we look at success and failure overall. We should begin by treating these two 'impostors' just the same, to paraphrase Rudyard Kipling.[6] I've tried to show why I don't believe there is much to be gained from analyzing triumphs. Next, I'll go one step further and argue we can earn more from failure than we can learn from success.

FOCUSING ON FAILURE INSTEAD OF STUDYING SUCCESS
As counterintuitive as this may sound, we need to devote more energy to figuring out our failures. Why is that the case? First, errors are usually endemic: we tend to make the same mistakes instead of random ones. It can be something as innocuous as a penchant for going to the net in tennis behind a weak serve, or more ominous behavior like sabotaging your career by being a boor towards your boss. Either way, most of us are guilty of repeating both big and small blunders. This often happens because the errors we make are rooted in deep-seated issues as difficult to excavate as they are to exterminate. We'll explore this further in a future chapter, but the key takeaway is while successes come in large part by **chance**, failures are almost always the product of patterns.

This is one of the advantages of concentrating on when and why things go wrong. Because mistakes are often systematic, they are also, to a certain extent, expected. In contrast to success, failure is predictable — and that can be of practical use. We should also realize that a corollary to failure's predictability is its consistency. Not only can we anticipate where people will make mistakes in the future based on their past, we should expect that they will. For example, why do we assume Wall Street banks will learn the lessons from the 2008 economic crisis, when they have never learned from previous crashes? If we're honest, we know these investment banks will, at some point, fuel other bubbles.

This could frustrate you, but it should also prompt you to try avoiding the mistake in the first place. If misfortune can, to a certain extent, be anticipated, wouldn't you want to take steps to avoid it? Of course you would — and you'd begin by looking more closely at when you've failed rather then when you've flourished.

We spend most of our time studying wins, but we are much more likely to benefit from examining losses. Triumph is like winning the lottery; yet disaster offers us more of a teachable moment. Remember also failure is more common, too: why study random, rare successes when their opposites are both more predictable and more prevalent? Unlike good outcomes, whose origins are often opaque, the root causes of setbacks are far easier to trace. They may be possible to sidestep in the future as a result. Success stories sell, but focusing on failure is a superior strategy for rapid, enduring improvement. The key to flipping the switch is in drawing the lessons from what drives them: our mistakes.

WHEN THE LIGHT BULB CAME ON
"Man approaches the unattainable truth through a succession of errors." **Aldous Huxley**

Before Thomas Edison was successful in perfecting the product that would literally light up the world, he tried two thousand different materials in search of a filament for the light bulb. When none worked satisfactorily, his assistant complained, "All our work is in vain. We have learned nothing."

Edison replied very confidently, "we have come a long way and we have learned a lot. We know that there are two thousand elements we cannot use to make a good light bulb ... Negative results are just what I want. They're as valuable to me as positive results. I can never find the thing that does the job best until I find the ones that don't." He added, "I haven't failed. I've just found 10,000 ways that won't work."

Edison's career spanned six decades, where his businesses and products — inventions as varied as the first movie camera and the phonograph, the precursor to the record player — changed life as we know it. When he died he held the world record for patents, a topic on which he once mused: "I make more mistakes than anyone else I know, and sooner or later I patent most of them."

MAGNIFICENT MISTAKES | THE DISCOVERY OF VIAGRA

Description: Viagra is one of the world's most-prescribed drugs. In its first decade on the market, it was prescribed to 30 million men in over 120 countries. It represents one of the greatest pharmaceutical successes of the past 50 years; but did you know it began as a failure?

What Went Wrong? Researchers at Pfizer were looking for a drug to treat angina, a condition that constricts the heart's blood vessels. The experimental drug showed little promise in dealing with that problem, but scientists were surprised to learn of its now-famous side effect of combating erectile dysfunction.

Lesson Learned: Viagra was an "accidental discovery" as were penicillin, pasteurization and Post-It Notes. The history of science is full of similarly serendipitous observations leading to groundbreaking products, theories and treatments.

Don't be so quick to dismiss a "failure" at first glance; how might you repurpose it to meet another need?

It should come as no surprise that managing mistakes is a key part of progress in science. What about in the rest of life? Is correcting your errors a great way to improve your life, career or business as it was for Thomas Edison and his light bulb? The short answer is yes, and we'll devote a good chunk of this book to exploring the many examples of this power law. But first, we need to understand why learning from such failures is the only way to build the foundation for future triumphs.

THE UPSIDE OF ERROR

Nature provides us with perhaps the best example of the benefits of mistakes. After all, the most powerful force at play in that sphere — evolution — emerges from nature's flaws and the consequences they make.

The process of evolution can be crudely summarized as follows: Humans, plants and animals experience random genetic mutations from generation to generation. These changes produce specific heritable traits that make it more likely for that organism to successfully reproduce in the future, thus becoming more common in a population over time. Eventually, these species evolve to all possess the beneficial trait that was the unexpected 'gift' of the earlier genetic mutation.

I just tried to condense Charles Darwin's *On the Origin of Species* into three sentences. However, the most important point is this: evolution is powered by happy accidents. Mutations — the building block of genetic adaption — are nothing more than programming errors occurring in our DNA. Seen from this light, 'learning' from mistakes is truly the most elementary feedback loop in nature. Species experience genetic errors that either advance or handicap successful reproduction; the system learns by selecting the beneficial genes and discarding the unfavorable ones.

We need to return to that organic perspective on
mistakes — one that sees them as opportunities for growth
and evolution rather than decline and decay.

FAILURE IS ESSENTIAL TO SUCCESS
Thomas Watson believed in the benefits of failing. The founder of computer giant IBM had a legendary affinity for mistakes, and even made committing them a core element of his
business philosophy. "The way to succeed," he used to say, "is
to double your error rate." Watson understood groundbreaking success could not be achieved by playing it safe, and a company could only make significant strides by running the risk
of repeated, though small, setbacks. These days, it's common
to speak of companies that have become 'too big to fail.' What
Watson and others might argue is these institutions became
big precisely *by* failing, early and often. This is as true in life
as it is in business; as filmmaker Woody Allen likes to note,
"if you're not failing every now and again, it's a sure sign that
you're not trying anything very innovative."

The flamboyant British billionaire Richard Branson —
founder of all things Virgin — underscored this when he
noted "you don't learn to walk by following rules. You learn
by doing, and by falling over." Another reason is more pedagogical, if not psychological. Quite simply, disappointment is
a better teacher than triumph. Setbacks sting and sear, burn-
ing hard-earned lessons into memory, in a way that successes
don't.

This is, in part, because of our hard wiring towards loss-
aversion instead of gain-maximization. As humans, we've
evolved to recoil from, recall and often regret losses to an almost irrational extent — so much so that this tendency will

THE MAGNIFICENT MISTAKE

distort our behavior when choosing between alternatives. Emotions are asymmetric; studies have shown negative feelings are longer lasting and more powerful than positive ones. We therefore prioritize avoiding pain over seeking pleasure in making decisions, but this bias affects us retrospectively as well. In a nutshell, we are bruised by losses but we have a tendency to become blasé about successes. Anybody who has ever gone through a romantic break-up can attest to how heartache can leave a scar; but while we might have warm memories of falling in love with someone, somehow those recalled emotions aren't as intense.

Errors therefore serve as exceptional teachable moments. Great politicians, for example, are almost always marked by an early loss that ultimately leads to later electoral success.

Many occupants of the Oval Office can point to near-death political experiences as crucial turning points in their careers. George W. Bush was haunted by both his failed run for a seat in the US House of Representatives in 1978, as well as his father's loss to Bill Clinton in the 1992 presidential campaign. Even a political prodigy like Barack Obama has been bruised by a campaign setback. Before his meteoric rise to the US Senate in 2004 and his election to the presidency four years later, Obama failed in his attempt to unseat Congressman Bobby Rush in 2000. In his book *The Bridge*, Obama biographer David Remnick called the future president's only loss a political lesson. "In any great career, failure is an instructive moment. That was his," Remnick noted.[8]

This phenomenon is not confined to business or politics. J.K. Rowling, author of the extraordinarily successful *Harry Potter* book and film franchise, spoke of the 'fringe benefits of failure' in a 2008 commencement address at Harvard

University. After detailing how she reached rock bottom and having "failed on an epic scale" in her early life, Rowling went on to describe what those defeats did for her:

> "Some failure in life is inevitable. It is impossible to live without failing at something, unless you live so cautiously that you might as well not have lived at all — in which case, you have failed ... Failure taught me things about myself that I could have learned no other way ... The knowledge that you have emerged wiser and stronger from setbacks means that you are, ever after, secure in your ability to survive ... Such knowledge is a true gift, for all that is painfully won, and it has been worth more than any qualification that I ever earned."[9]

MAGNIFICENT MISTAKES | BILL CLINTON'S FIRST LOSS

Description: Bill Clinton, while basking in the glory of being elected America's youngest governor in 1978 (in Arkansas), became the country's youngest ex-governor two years later.

What Went Wrong? Clinton underestimated the anger an unpopular motor vehicle tax would cause. Voters punished what seemed like hubris from a young, ambitious politician by turning him out of office after just one term.

Lesson Learned: Clinton mourned that loss deeply, but also sought to learn from it. He asked friends and foes alike why he had lost. He absorbed the error of his ways and resolved to do things differently if he got another chance. According to his biographer David Maraniss that defeat chastened him enough to catapult him to reelection to the governorship in 1982 and, ten years later, to the White

House.[7] ***Errors can define your epitaph or they can be springboards to future success.***

Finally, failing can be very motivational. You would think that getting cut from your high school basketball team at fourteen might discourage you from expecting to play in college, let alone having a career in the NBA. Tell that to Michael Jordan, who used the setback as a springboard, first as a star at the University of North Carolina and subsequently in becoming the greatest professional basketball player of all time. In fact, Jordan has said his accomplishments were inspired by those disappointments, not achieved in spite of them: "I've failed over and over and over again in my life," he once remarked, "and that is why I succeed."[10]

Blunders can lead to new beginnings and even better performances later. They teach us we can survive stumbles, overcome misfortune and emerge more confident and aware of our abilities. While this is true for individuals, it is equally so for companies and even entire industries, which are predicated on systematic failure.

WINNING BY LOSING

"Baseball is the only field of endeavor where a man can succeed three times out of ten and be considered a good performer." **Ted Williams**

The late Ted Williams of the Boston Red Sox is widely considered to be one of the greatest hitters in the history of Major League Baseball. His career batting average of .344 is seventh on the all-time list, and fellow legend Joe DiMaggio declared Williams "was the best pure hitter I ever saw."

Williams' *bona fides* as a prolific batter are beyond question. However, as he liked to point out, his strikeouts at the plate came more frequently than his successes. Even with one of the highest batting averages of all time, Williams didn't get a hit six times out of every ten at bat.[11]

Surprisingly, a lot of life is just like baseball. For individuals and institutions alike, setbacks are expected, even factored in to the calculus of eventual success. In these areas of activity, frustrations are a part of the process — an inevitable by-product of the road to fame and fortune.

The venture capital industry is just such a field. High stakes capital funding of fledgling start-ups is, by definition, a volatile and risky proposition. Indeed, most investments do not meet expectations. The failure rates of these firms can be surprisingly high. Anywhere from 20% to 90% of the enterprises funded do not return the invested amounts. Yet venture capitalists survive and even thrive, by learning how to effectively manage their risks while hitting the occasional home run.

MAGNIFICENT MISTAKES | DECCA RECORDS AND "THE DEATH OF GUITAR MUSIC"

Description: In January 1962, an executive at the Decca Recording Company listened to a fifteen-song set from an up-and-coming four-man band.

What Went Wrong? After listening to the audition, the executive rejected the band, saying: "we don't like their sound, and guitar music is on the way out." The name of the executive: unknown; the name of the band he rejected? The Beatles.

Lesson Learned: This could be considered one of the biggest blunders of all time. It's unkind to be so harsh in hindsight, but the fact remains Decca horribly miscalculated the future of musical tastes. It is also surprising, considering they were one of the top two record labels in Britain at the time. Thus even organizations at the top of their

game make mistakes, and some turn out to be monumental ones.
Keep this in mind the next time you screw up: at least you didn't
reject the Beatles.

This could just as easily be applied to any hit-driven industry
where flops are more frequent than successes. Film studios
and music labels make many of the same bets venture capitalists do, often with even higher miss-to-hit ratios. Yet they don't
dwell on their box office bombs (unless they are colossal, like
John Carter or *The Lone Ranger*) and take those setbacks in
stride.

They limit their mistakes, to be sure. But they have also
accepted errors are part of the territory — a necessary cost of
doing business in their industry. It's precisely this equanim-
ity towards false steps as demonstrated by successful investors
and movie studios we should all adopt.

DON'T JUST LIMIT YOUR MISTAKES — PROFIT FROM THEM

Why have I gone to such great lengths to describe the upside
of errors, how failure is essential to success, and how great
performers and profitable businesses alike lose more often
than they win? Because I want to change the way we look at
mistakes. In fact, I want to reverse the received wisdom entirely. Errors offer great opportunities in disguise, if we have
the courage and capacity to make the most of them. Failing to
take advantage of our stumbles is itself a missed opportunity.
This isn't a purely philosophical observation, but a practical
one as well. We need to change the conversation from one
focused solely on success to one that also explores the fruits
of failure. Mistakes count — more than you realize. Errors
often, if not always, determine outcomes. We know this to be

particularly true in sports, politics and in business, to name but three fields of competition.

In certain athletic activities such as gymnastics or figure skating, mistakes mean everything when it comes to assessing performance. In these realms, she or he who makes the fewest miscues wins. Some sports have even coined specific phrases to capture the significance of blunders; thus, tennis analysts keep track of unforced errors, while football commentators preach about the importance of avoiding interceptions and turnovers. Lou Holtz, a coach who had enormous success at both the college and professional football levels, has gone so far as to say: "coaching is nothing more than eliminating mistakes before you get fired."

It's also the case that many political races are lost more than won, as a cynical electorate no longer votes for a candidate so much as against their opponent. The rise of negative ads, and their predominance in political campaigns in the past decades, demonstrates the power of framing your opponent in an unflattering light.

In the increasingly zero-sum, I-win-you-lose world we live in, errors are often all that separates the victor and the vanquished. Napoleon understood this all too well, remarking "the greatest general is he who makes the fewest mistakes" and "never interrupt your enemy when he is making a mistake."

To be fair, mistakes have always mattered; we have simply forgotten this power law of history too many times. However, it seems as though today we are also making more of them than ever before. Moreover, no mess-ups are 'small' anymore. If one thinks back over the past decade — from the management of Hurricane Katrina or the ongoing humanitarian crisis in Syria, to the housing bubble that led to the Great

Recession of 2008 and the failure to spot the Bernard Madoff Ponzi scheme — those missteps have not just been utter embarrassments; they've impacted cities, countries and the entire global economy with monumental consequences. There should be a real urgency to tame mistakes today, given the enormous stakes at play.

Perhaps the most frustrating aspect of this increasing 'errorism' is so many of them are avoidable. The key is not only in learning from our mistakes, which we all intuitively understand we should do. It should also be to stop making the same ones repeatedly.

Finally, one can't, of course, simply 'reverse' a mistake. You can't alter the past, or the fact you erred in the first place, but you *can* change the legacy of that miscue. By learning from your errors, you can increase the chances you won't repeat them. In my experience, most mistakes are entirely avoidable because we have been down that road before, or one that looks like it. To paraphrase Mark Twain, errors may not always repeat themselves exactly, but they often rhyme.

In some ways, people are just like hardened, career criminals: they have a high recidivism rate for messing up. Occasionally, this is because people don't know they've committed an error; call it blissful ignorance. In other instances, we don't have the courage to face up to a failure, for the simple reason we would have to accept responsibility for the outcome. Perhaps most frustrating, there are those who *know* they repeatedly make mistakes and yet refuse to change their behavior — as if they were entirely powerless to do so. The great Albert Einstein had these people in mind when he said the definition of insanity was "doing the same thing over and over again and expecting different results."

Let me be clear here: I am not advocating we strive to never commit an error. In fact, it's just the opposite: I embrace mistakes. However, I am opposed to repeat (and therefore preventable) ones. Wrong decisions are an inevitable part of life. But bad decisions — making an errant step when we know better — are unforced errors.

CRACKING THE "TALENT CODE"

In 2009, journalist Daniel Coyle published a groundbreaking book that revolutionized thinking about how talent develops. Like most people, I assumed extraordinary people were simply born that way, and their greatness was largely a genetic gift. I had it all wrong.

Recent scientific discoveries have demonstrated there is a precise formula for building expertise. New insights into the way the human mind develops skills have focused on a neural layer in the brain called myelin, which is the critical link to the process.

As Coyle explains in *The Talent Code*, "every human skill, whether it's playing baseball or playing Bach, is created by a chain of nerve fibers carrying a tiny electrical impulse — basically, a signal traveling through a circuit. Myelin's vital role is to wrap those nerve fibers the same way rubber insulation wraps a copper wire, making the signal stronger and faster by preventing the electrical impulses from leaking out. When we fire our circuits in the right way — when we practice swinging that bat or playing that note — our myelin responds by wrapping layers around that neural circuit, each new layer adding a bit more skill and speed. The thicker the myelin gets, the better it insulates, and the faster and more accurate our movements and thoughts become."[12]

But what does this have to do with mistakes, you ask? The key is a concept known as 'deliberate practice.' Most people intuitively accept we get good at something through repetition; practice makes perfect, after all. However, simply rehearsing a movement over and over again does not, in and of itself, develop mastery. Rather, our mind and muscles require a certain type of practice where we are constantly being challenged to raise our game, and most importantly when we commit and receive immediate feedback on the making of mistakes. Through this specific activity, our brains rewire themselves by adding successive layers of myelin around the neural circuits, constantly optimizing the movement or memory — and developing expertise in the process. If you wanted to distill skill building into an equation, this might be how it would look:

Skill = Deliberate Practice x Time
(10,000 hours, or 10 years)

Deliberate Practice = Time x (Making and Correcting Mistakes)

Deliberate practice, in Coyle's view, is "not ordinary practice. This is something else: a highly targeted, error-focused process." In other words, as he puts it, in order to "practice more deeply, [one needs to] struggle, make errors, and learn from them."

While the scientific insights of this research are fascinating in and of themselves, the real-world implications are nothing less than paradigm shifting: we now know beyond a shadow of a doubt mistakes are actually indispensable parts of developing expertise.

THE LAST WORD

To become great at something — anything — one cannot afford to ignore errors. The story of Thomas Edison teaches us the importance of tolerating mistakes as the price of progress, in science, as was in his case, but equally in almost every other aspect of life. However, recent discoveries in neuroscience indicate we can't simply settle for accepting them as a 'cost of doing business'. In fact, the key to one critical element to improving performance in any area is actually to take notice of those mistakes, find them and fix them. Wisdom acquired through mistakes is both learned and earned.

I am willing to go one step further. I believe learning from mistakes is the secret to long-term success, and we will spend the next chapter discovering just how many of the world's top performing individuals and organizations have been using this little known formula all along.

Chapter One - The Speed Read

In a nutshell:

Successes come in large part by *chance*; failures are almost always the product of patterns. Mistakes can therefore be tracked and fixed.

Wrong decisions are an inevitable part of life. But bad decisions — making an errant step when we know better — are unforced errors. There is nothing remotely redeemable about making the same mistake twice.

Wisdom acquired through mistakes is both learned and earned. Perhaps the most important change we can make to improve our performance is to consistently learn from our mistakes.

Points to Ponder:

✔ Mistakes don't so much teach the lessons your *want* as the ones you *need*.

✔ Success is often surprising, serendipitous and spontaneous. It is also often the sum of a series of small, steady steps, as opposed to the result of some single, seismic event. Failure, on the other hand, is predictable and systematic.

✔ Skill = Deliberate Practice x Time (10,000 hours, or 10 years), and Deliberate Practice = Time x (Making and Correcting Mistakes)

✔ In order to become great at something — anything — one cannot afford to ignore errors. In fact, it is the opposite: the critical element of the process is actually to take notice of those mistakes, find them and fix them.

PUTTING IT INTO PRACTICE > ASK YOURSELF:

- How do you react when you make a mistake? Do you see it as a necessary step along the way to success, or do you let it stop you in your tracks?
- Do you think that you learn from your mistakes?
- What was your biggest mistake, and what exactly did you learn from it? How did you learn from it?
- Is there an area in your life where you have been applying some 'deliberate practice' to improve your game, performance or skill level? Or have you just been repeating the same mistakes?

2

WHO:

**TURNING ERRORS INTO EXCELLENCE | THE SIMPLE SECRET
BEHIND SOME OF THE WORLD'S TOP ORGANIZATIONS**

"If you don't make mistakes, you can't make decisions." **Warren
Buffett, Chairman and CEO, Berkshire Hathaway**

W arren Buffett is one of the world's richest people.
The man they call "the Oracle from Omaha"
has built a well-earned reputation as a legendary
stock picker, and his Delphic pronouncements on investments
are always scrutinized, often acted upon and occasionally me-
morialized. There is good reason for that: over a half-century
in the game, he has made nearly $100 billion in equity invest-
ments and rarely put a foot wrong. Perhaps more than any
other individual investor in history, Warren Buffett is almost
always right ... but even *he* occasionally makes a mistake. And,
believe it or not, sometimes even two at the same time.

In 1993, Buffett spotted what he believed was a great deal: Dexter Shoe Company, a company nestled in the eponymous Maine town that had been making and selling sailing shoes for over 40 years. Dexter had ridden the wave of those models, made popular in the 1980s, to build a thriving business; it was now poised to rise to even higher levels of profitability. Buffett thought so too, and scooped up the company for $433 million.

The normally flawless Buffett made the first of two uncharacteristic miscalculations. On the one hand, he misread Dexter's position in the marketplace; as he later pointed out "what I had assessed as durable competitive advantage vanished within a few years."

This, in and of itself, would not turn out to be his main mistake. $433 million (what Buffett and his company, Berkshire Hathaway, paid for Dexter) is a lot of money to you and me, but seasoned equity investors like him can absorb such setbacks and do so from time to time. However, Buffett's blunder in buying the soon-to-be-almost valueless company was compounded by the fact he did so, atypically, with Berkshire stock. When Dexter was ultimately folded into another holding company in 2001, the appreciation in the corresponding value of Berkshire shares attributed to Dexter's purchase turned the $433 million price into a $3.5 billion write-down.[1]

The Dexter acquisition stands, by Buffett's own admission, as the worst business error he ever committed. In fact, it may have been the most expensive one in history. But what separates Warren Buffett from other, less successful investors is not the mistakes he makes, but what he makes of them.

Warren Buffett did not hide from this colossal lapse in financial judgment; in fact, he talked about it, openly, in his annual letter to Berkshire shareholders a few years later. Not only did he take full responsibility for the miscalculation by stating: "to date, Dexter is the worst deal that I've made". He also went on: "I'll make more mistakes in the future — you can bet on that." Buffett also accepted the inevitably of making them, pointing out that "if you don't make mistakes, you can't make decisions."[2]

Warren Buffett demonstrates an enlightened and ultimately enormously successful perspective on errors. He concedes that they're a part of life, accepts the need to own up to them, and perhaps most importantly recognizes the value in learning from them. As he is fond of saying, "you need not focus on your mistakes any more than necessary to learn their lessons" and "you want to learn from experience, but you want to learn from other people's experience when you can."[3]

One of the best-kept secrets of truly successful people and organizations is they systematically learn from their mistakes.

This chapter looks at how top-performing institutions tackle failure. We'll examine first how some of the world's best companies consistently address errors in a systematic effort to learn the right lessons from them. Then we will study the U.S. Army and the Israeli Air Force to demonstrate how this best practice exists beyond the business world. In the end, we'll see the common bond between top-tier companies like Amazon and sporting champions such as Ayrton Senna is they intentionally and relentlessly learn from their mistakes.

BUSINESS

CASE STUDY I: AMAZON.COM

"Obstacles are only obstacles if you think they're obstacles. Otherwise, they're opportunities." **Jeff Bezos, founder and CEO, Amazon.com**

If there is one company that is the epitome of the Internet era, it may very well be Amazon. Started as an almost quixotic quest by Jeff Bezos in 1995, the company has grown, in less than two decades, into the world's largest online retailer. Today, it serves over 200 million customers, generates over $60 billion a year in revenues, and is poised to be the principal e-commerce player of the twenty-first century. As a recent *Fast Company* article proclaimed, "Amazon has done a lot more than become a stellar retailer. It has reinvented, disrupted, redefined and renovated the global marketplace."

Like Warren Buffett's Berkshire Hathaway, it is one of the world's most valuable companies; and, like Buffett, its CEO Bezos owes at least some measure of that success to his attention to mistakes. In contrast to Buffett's homespun attitude towards error, however, Amazon has developed a systematic approach it rolls out at every opportunity.

The CoE

When a big mess-up occurs, Amazon relies on a little publicized but often used process known to employees as the CoE: the Collection of Errors.[4] This protocol is principally triggered by any site outage, which would be considered a critical breakdown for an online retailer. I've included a portion of the guidelines below in significant detail, because I believe it's the clearest way to demonstrate how seriously Amazon approaches error analysis:

Amazon CoE-Guidelines from Amazon HQ Wiki
1 Friday Availability Review
    2 Key Elements
    3 Analysis
    3.1 5 Whys - Exposing elements of the Failure Chain (Width Analysis)
    3.2 5 Whys - Getting to Root Cause (Depth Analysis)
    3.3 What is an Actionable Root Cause?
    3.4 What isn't a root cause?
    3.5 Example
    4 Time Line
    5 Actions & Prevention
    Best practice is to complete the CoE draft within 24-48 hours of the event while the details are still fresh.

Key Elements
Short description: This is how you would summarize the event in 2 min or less. A more verbose description or narrative can also be included.

    Analysis: This is boiling down the event into what failed, went wrong, complicated detection or resolution of the event, etc ... Think of it like you are creating a series of Cliff notes to allow for the reader to quickly grok the key elements of the event.

    Timeline: List the times of important events of the timeline.

    Lessons learned: Things we learned and people should take away from the event.

    Actions: What needs to be done to prevent or fix what failed or went wrong.

5 Whys - Exposing elements of the Failure Chain (Width)
When conducting the analysis of an event — it is useful to capture the questions that expose key elements in the failure chain that caused, could have prevented, or were reactive symptoms of the event. These are the top-level questions that drive analysis such as:
Why did the event occur?
Why was the time between defect introduction and problem detection so long?

5 Whys - Getting to Root Cause (Analysis Depth)
The application of the 5 Whys methodology to these questions can lead to a deeper analysis and root cause of each symptom of the event.

As you can see, Amazon doesn't mess around with their mistakes. The protocol is also used anytime there is a problem that is customer facing or affecting customer satisfaction. Mechanisms are then put in place to avoid those errors in the future. Amazon is a very data-driven company, and senior managers are always diving into the metrics to see how they're performing. The CoE is an example of how seriously the organization takes customer-facing breakdowns, and it has to be looked at in the context of Amazon's path to corporate prominence.

From the very beginning, Jeff Bezos understood the website experience was the storefront of the business. Amazon launched its website in the summer of 1995. As one observer pointed out, "in many ways Amazon's early design was a combination of trial and error, good guessing, chance and some clever improvisations ... they paid attention to what customers liked and what they didn't." Even in those first days, Bezos had his programmers focus on making it the easiest and most useful website around — more useful, it was hoped, than shopping in the real world.

Amazon became an e-commerce behemoth, however, by rolling out innovation after innovation. From the One Click buy button to the recommendation algorithms almost every transactional website has copied today, Amazon's competitive advantage was painstakingly built, virtual brick by virtual brick. Not all of their new features stuck; but Bezos was canny enough to understand true improvement could only come out an environment where his team had the freedom to fail. That uncommon openness would show in other ways.

Complaints are opportunities to improve

How important is it to Amazon that the organization is always learning from its errors? No mistake is too small to escape their attention. Customers can email Jeff Bezos directly, and all of his email is read. This is not a public relations exercise, either. In his book on Amazon, *One Click*, author Richard Brandt retells the story of how, early on in the company's development, an elderly lady emailed Bezos to say that she loved ordering from Amazon but had to have her nephew come over each time to open the package. He promptly had the boxes redesigned.[5]

Amazon executives have caught Bezos drifting off in meetings because he gets so caught up in reading complaints. As a *Fortune* magazine article on the company described, "those e-mails trigger what Amazon people call a Jeff B. escalation." One senior manager confessed this focus on small errors was not always understood at first. "My initial reaction was: 'You want me to be working on a Friday night on an order that was messed up by half a day?' Then it sank in. If one customer wrote to Jeff, there are others who didn't. And Jeff wants to understand the screw-up to make sure it gets fixed." That same spirit animates the company almost two decades after its founding.

The pursuit of perfection

Today, Amazon powers its massive retail business in part by the flawless execution of picking and packing the products it ships from its warehouses. While it is increasingly automated, real people are still very much involved in that system, not least in thinking of new ways to make the end-to-end process more efficient. Teams are constantly tweaking the fulfillment chain — eliminating wasteful movements, creating synergies, and especially reducing errors. Thanks to this relentless focus on process improvement, delivery times today are 25% faster than they were just two years ago.

This extraordinary system was not always a part of the master plan. In fact, it's yet another example of how Bezos turned an early miscalculation into an eventual asset. From the beginning, he had always hoped the company would carry no inventory, simply acting as a conduit between consumers and distributors. As the business grew, however, he realized he also had to control that piece of the value chain. As he put it, "the logistics of distribution are the iceberg below the waterline of online book selling." What's more, he felt he could improve the speed, efficiency and customer experience by taking over that part of the process. People could now get their products faster, more cheaply, and track the parcels as they made their way to them. When Jeff Bezos learns from a mistake, he doubles down on the lesson learned: after resisting the idea entirely, Amazon today has positioned 89 giant ful-fillment centers around the globe.

The reason he did so was simple: because it would im-prove the value proposition to his customers. Since its found-ing, Bezos has made customer service the cornerstone of Amazon's strategy. His goal was "to create the world's most consumer-centric company." As one person familiar with how Amazon operates pointed out, they don't worry about getting better vis-à-vis our competitors; they worry, as Bezos is fond of saying, about "getting better and better for our customers." This idea of constant improvement is encoded in the DNA of their corporate culture: Amazonians believe the company is always either improving or declining. Quite simply, there is no standing still.

Capitalizing on competitors' self-inflicted wounds

Amazon does not stop at limiting its own mistakes; it has also proven adept at exploiting other companies' errors. Perhaps their boldest stroke in this vein was to persuade their bricks and mortar rival, Borders, to outsource their earliest e-com-merce activities to them.

This turned out to be a titanic mistake. As Ajaz Ahmed and Stefan Olander point out in their book, *Velocity: The Seven New Laws For a World Gone Digital*:

"Short term, it was convenient ... Long term, it was fatal, as Borders never took the necessary steps to transform the orga-nization so that the digital world became a true core compe-tence of their business."[6]

Borders realized its blunder, but too late. It reclaimed its online fulfillment in 2007, but the damage had already been done. The 40-year-old company filed for bankruptcy 4 years later, in large part because it had been outflanked online by its youthful competitor.

Learning from others' mistakes: the Kindle

The company's biggest innovation to date was born, at least in part, by the mistakes their competitors made, as well as the moves they failed to make. Bezos saw what Amazon did to Borders ... and wondered what could upend his company? One of the few threats to an online retailer of books, he realized, would be the emergence of electronic media. Unlike his competition, Bezos didn't wait for the change to happen, though; in 2007, he effectively launched the e-book industry with the release of the Kindle e-reader.

The decision to cannibalize his own sales was a direct response to the lessons learned, the hard way, by the failure to do so by Borders and Barnes and Noble. Amazon drew from the mistakes of their competition, to be sure. But with the Kindle, they also improved upon the earlier e-readers that had come out — and failed miserably — before it.

The first e-book readers had many flaws; they were too expensive, too big and too clunky. So Amazon sold the first Kindles at a loss, worked on their form factor, and made the reading experience on their device more pleasant by investing in the development of electronic ink. Bezos improved the hardware, but crucially he also invested in the ecosystem that supported it.

The biggest reason for the flop of early e-readers, however, was there were too few digital titles to feed the platform.

Amazon made sure there'd be a critical mass of e-books available (over 90,000) at its launch in order to make the purchase of a Kindle worthwhile.

The Kindle changed everything. It was the starting gun to the e-book revolution and almost certainly influenced the development and release of another game-changing electronic device, the iPad. Today, the Kindle is on its fourth release and the industry it helped create is slated to be worth $3 billion annually by 2015. Amazingly, Amazon now sells more e-books than real books — almost 400 million in 2012 — and analysts estimate they own 45% of the global market.

Far from perfect, but perfectly adaptive

The first person Jeff Bezos hired at Amazon remarked the company believed in a "bias for action … we tried a lot of things and made a lot of mistakes, but managed to avoid any fatal ones."[7] Amazon's story is not an uninterrupted litany of victories, to be sure. The company has experienced its fair share of setbacks. Among them, it tried to copy Google (with its own search engine, A9) and eBay (with Amazon Auctions) and failed miserably. It saw its stock price drop from $100 at its zenith to $6 at its lows. It went through its first six full years before finally posting a profit. However, it has not only endured these travails; it has extracted wisdom from them.

That is one of the undeniable keys to their success. It has become a conscious part of its corporate culture, and the rigorous analysis of mistakes is through the CoE has become an institutional reflex. The innovative attitude towards error goes further than that, however: they have intentionally created an environment where innovations, even if they fail at first, are encouraged. Amazon also ruthlessly exploits their competitors' mistakes, while simultaneously heeding their warnings.

This openness is also a function of the man who leads the company. As one business profile put it, their CEO "is persistent, tenacious, and adaptive." If that sounds like a perfect formula for turning obstacles into opportunities, you're right. Jeff Bezos and Amazon have dreamt big, dared to fail, dusted themselves off after every setback, and developed a culture and system to consistently draw lessons from each one of them.

MAGNIFICENT MISTAKES | AMAZON'S BIGGEST BLUNDER
Description: In 2009, Amazon tried to undo the fact that it had sold an unlicensed digital copy of a book by secretly removing it from the files of multiple Kindle users.

What Went Wrong? Amazon made a small mistake much bigger by being seen as invading the "privacy" of people's digital libraries. Taking back the book from people's collections overnight hurt Amazon's trust level with customers. Amazon prides itself on being a customer-centric company, and this one ill-considered act eroded the trust it took Amazon years to build with its consumers. Almost immediately, the company apologized for the unauthorized deletion and resolved to never unilaterally rescind a purchase like that again.

Lesson Learned: They took steps to make sure this could never happen again — or violate the customer's trust in the same way. Jeff Bezos and Amazon have made mistakes — lots of them. This was the biggest to date, but not their only one.

They unsuccessfully tried to compete with eBay through Amazon Auctions, for example. The company is willing to make mistakes in the name of innovation while being systematic about quickly correcting and learning from them. Their rapid reaction to the error — and the reversal of the policy — restored some of the trust they had lost in the incident. However, they have a knack for mitigating those mistakes, then making sure that they never happen again. **Successful companies like Amazon have carefully considered plans for dealing with failures.**

It might be tempting to think only technology companies can benefit from focusing on fixing mistakes. This could not be more wrong. While Amazon has had great success in the technology space doing so, perhaps the organization most associated with this practice excels in 'old-world' manufacturing. That company is Toyota, and it is responsible for introducing a Japanese concept — *Kaizen* — into the worldwide business lexicon.

CASE STUDY II: TOYOTA
"Problems must be made visible." **Katsuaki Watanabe, President, Toyota Motor Corporation**

In 2008, Toyota Motor Corporation (Toyota) achieved a milestone few ever thought possible: it supplanted General Motors (GM) as the world's largest automobile manufacturer. Their perch atop the automotive world didn't last long, however; by 2009, Toyota found itself at the centre of biggest product recall in a decade, and in the midst of a public relations disaster that would only be eclipsed by GM's recall crisis a few years later.

After years of corporate soul-searching as well as millions of car recalls, Toyota seems to have righted the ship. It has also begun to gain back the reputation for reliability it has so carefully cultivated over 4 decades, and win back customers in the process: by 2014, Toyota had regained the top spot as the globe's biggest car company.

Correcting course for Toyota wasn't easy, but it also wasn't surprising: over the last 40 years — and before the 2009 safety recalls — it had become widely regarded as one of the world's best-run companies.

For almost all of its history, the Toyota brand had been synonymous with quality. In fact, an astonishing 80% of all Toyotas sold in the US in the past two decades are still on the road today, according to one of their senior executives. That their once-sterling reputation could suffer such a setback is further proof that success can be surprisingly temporary. Toyota stopped doing some of the things that had sustained their rise for so long. How had they managed such a long-standing focus on excellence? Journalist David Magee, who wrote a book on Toyota[8], believes he knows why:

"During its ascent, Toyota has had the reputation of being invincible, a corporation that rarely missteps, while its competitors have made multiple high-profile mistakes through the years … Toyota has avoided the really major gaffes — debacles like Ford's Pinto and the Explorer/Firestone tire controversy, and General Motors' periodic financial meltdowns over the past two decades. It's not that Toyota doesn't make mistakes — far from it. The difference, though, is how Toyota typically responds to the mere hint of a problem."

Jim Press, President of Toyota's North America division, provided even more insight into their approach to error when he stated flatly: "You don't learn from success; mistakes are what shapes us. We treasure mistakes."

Toyota had clearly gone off course in making the series of mistakes that led to the 2009 product recalls, but luckily they already had the system, and the culture, in place to bounce back from those setbacks. In the end, Toyota was able to recover from what could have been fatal blows to their brand, and it is due in large measure to how they have always — except for this one ignominious counter-example — attacked failure.

Toyota, like Amazon, consciously views miscues as invaluable learning opportunities. In fact, they make a point of calling immediate attention to defects. Every Toyota assembly line around the world has the so-called andon cords ('andon' comes from the Japanese word for 'lamp') arrayed along them so any employee can stop the entire production cycle if they spot a threat to product quality. Then "once a problem is identified, team members work together to fully flesh out and fix the mistake, so quality can be quickly restored."

Toyota's approach is such they cannot learn from mistakes until they identify and then fix them. The andon cord system reinforces the first step in the process; to borrow a phrase from the U.S. Homeland Security Department, Toyota employees have a responsibility to say something if they see something.

But how, exactly, do they implement this unique corporate practice of learning from mistakes after spotting them? It all starts with the TPS: the Toyota Production System.

The TPS
TPS is at the core of how Toyota operates. More than a formula, it's a culture as well as a set of guiding principles permeating every aspect of the company. It's also widely considered to be the principal source of competitive advantage for Toyota in the global automobile industry. Finally, it's arguably the most studied and emulated corporate practice in modern business history.

TPS is built on two main principles:

1) *Just-in-time* manufacturing — reducing wasteful inventory by using only 'what is needed, when it is needed, and in the amount needed.'

2) *Jidoka* — the ability to stop production lines to ensure quality.

The first element of their system, just-in-time inventory management, prompted a revolution in the way all companies manufacture goods now. It is a singular achievement in and of itself; however, for the purposes of our subject, it is the second principle that is of greater importance.

Jidoka, Hansei and Kaizen

Implementing the *Jidoka* value in Toyota's corporate culture means every employee not only can and must stop the manufacturing process as soon as they discover a mistake. Think, for a moment, what the implications of that philosophy are for the line worker on the shop floor: they are treated as responsible and excellent employees if they draw attention to an error. This culture of accountability is completely the opposite approach to those found in most corporate environments today, and it's a huge reason why Toyota has maintained its product quality, and top spot, for so long.

It's not enough to intentionally create a workplace that readily identifies mistakes. This is why two other important Japanese concepts underpin *Jidoka* at Toyota: the twin practices of *Hansei* and *Kaizen*. *Hansei* in Japanese means 'relentless reflection' whereas *Kaizen* is their word for continuous improvement.

Through *Hansei* and *Kaizen*, Toyota employees and executives alike think deeply about how to improve each aspect of their production system. Everyone at Toyota lives and breathes *Kaizen*, and it's a fundamental part of their corporate culture. To cite but one manifestation of it in action, Toyota receives over half a million suggestions for improvement every year, an average of over 10 per employee.

Kaizen is a cornerstone of their value system. The complete definition of the term in its Toyota context is "the ongoing process of continuous improvement through the elimination of waste in the workplace."

Kaizen relies on three principles:
1) Process and results (not just results)
2) Systematic Thinking (seeing the big picture)
3) Non-blaming (because blame is wasteful)

The *Kaizen* practice flows seamlessly from the *Hansei* philosophy. In the latter, the emphasis is on identifying what went wrong, and on creating specific strategies for ensuring that it does not happen again. At Toyota, even if a project is successful, employees still must conduct a *hansei-kai* (reflection meeting) to review the whole process and look for areas of improvement.

Another reason for Toyota's success is it is consistently counter-intuitive. Whereas employees at most companies tend to focus on good news, the policy at Toyota is to report about problems *first*. In fact, one of the maxims managers live by in the company is "problems must be made visible" as Toyota President Katsuake Watanabe puts it. Unsurprisingly, there is a Japanese concept for this idea, too: it's called *Mieruka*, which means to bring problems or facts into the open.

Mieruka, Jidoka, Hansei and *Kaizen* are Japanese values that all reinforce the same message at Toyota. Everyone at the company has to be open about issues, should be constantly looking for opportunities for improvement, and they all have an unambiguous duty to identify and fix errors. It's clear their corporate culture lays the philosophical foundation for learning from their mistakes; however, just how do they execute it in practice?

Here again, Toyota has pioneered a process copied by manufacturers and new media companies alike. In fact, we've already encountered a top company that has followed Toyota's example; that organization is Amazon, and the investigative technique is the 5 Whys.

The 5 Whys

Originally employed by company engineers in product development, Toyota's 5 Whys became notable in the 1970s after manufacturing experts began studying the company's production methods. The technique has spread and evolved into other well-known processes such as Six Sigma, a Motorola-developed system for eliminating defects.

The 5 Whys approach is, on the surface, as simple as it seems: the goal is to ask 'why' over and over — and a minimum of 5 times — to get to the actual cause of the issue in question. As one expert put it, this "layered interrogation gets team members to think below the surface of a problem and consider the chain reaction of consequences that lead back to the originating source of trouble."

Once more, Toyota leans on Japanese concepts and culture to institutionalize this habit. When using the 5 Whys process, executives are encouraged to practice *Genchi Genbutsu*: go to the source to find the facts to make correct decisions.

This exhaustive exploration of the hidden problems in a given situation may have been pioneered by Toyota, but it has firmly taken root in engineering circles worldwide. Indeed, root cause analysis and the Fishbone diagrams they spawn is now a staple of every quality control initiative today.

Process makes perfect

After this deep dive into their processes, Toyota's ascent to one of world's biggest car manufacturers and leading companies comes as less of a surprise. They were first in their industry, and one of the best in any industry, to systematically develop the culture and capacity to learn from their mistakes. Their principal source of competitive advantage, the Toyota Production System, is the foundation for their success, and it is "implemented on a daily basis by employees who eliminate waste, point out problems and system weaknesses, and make firsthand observations and recommendations for improvement."

However, even Toyota could not rely on TPS alone to create the conditions for this type of positive feedback; instead, they also lean on unique corporate values — such as *Hansei*, *Kaizen*, *Jidoka*, and *Genchi Genbutsi*, as well as process innovations like the 5 Whys — to put this philosophy into practice. Their results speak for themselves, which is why other companies, both in their industry and outside, have taken note.

We've seen how Amazon and Toyota both make a conscious effort to capture the value from mistakes. Thus, it's not a coincidence these two companies are the leading lights in their respective industries, even though both have made their share of massive miscues. In fact, I believe there is a clear link between errors and excellence, and it's clearly demonstrated to be a best practice in the world of profits and losses. Indeed, many other organizations have been putting this philosophy into action for years. Moreover, one could argue that the stakes for these institutions are even higher than mere dollars and cents, since they involve life and limbs. I'm speaking of the military, and we will explore two examples in turn.

MAGNIFICENT MISTAKES | THE MISSED OPPORTUNITY TO LEARN FROM THE MAGINOT LINE

Description: After World War I, the French built a series of fortifications to defend against another German invasion. Called the Maginot Line after France's Minister of War at the time (André Maginot), it was made up of 108 forts strung at nine-mile intervals between the Ardennes Forest in the North and the border with Switzerland in the South. Germany launched the famous Blitzkrieg tank raid on May 10 1940 and invaded France from the North, bypassing the fortification completely and marching through the Netherlands, Belgium and Luxembourg instead.

What Went Wrong? Maginot and the French war planners didn't expect German Panzer tanks to be able to roll through forests, so stopping the fortification line before the Ardennes turned out to be a calamitous error.

*Lesson Learned: Armies tend to "fight the last war," and the Maginot Line is perhaps history's best example of this phenomenon. Generals and general managers alike know: **It's critical to learn the right lessons from a mistake.***

THE MILITARY

CASE STUDY I: THE US ARMY

The U.S. Army is the principal branch of the largest and most powerful armed forces in the history of the world. For over two centuries, it has been the central instrument of American national security and has been deployed from the Revolutionary

War of 1775 to the current conflicts in Iraq and Afghanistan. There is no more lethal fighting force on Earth.

The Army takes its job very seriously, as it should; nothing less than the lives of its service men and women, as well as the security of the United States, rest on its shoulders. As a result, the Army works constantly to refine and update its tactics, techniques and procedures. There is probably no organization anywhere that has thought more deeply about, nor devoted more resources to, the task of getting better. If Toyota lives and breathes *Kaizen* on an industrial level, the U.S. Army implements it on an even greater scale. It should surprise no one, then, that Army leaders have historically looked to their mistakes as rich sources of new wisdom. The main method they use to do so has become known as the After-Action Review (AAR).[9]

The After-Action Review (AAR)

"When things don't go quite the way they intended, intelligent leaders are confident enough to step back and ask, 'why did things turn out that way?' Then they are smart enough to build on their strengths and avoid making the same mistake again." Excerpt from **Be, Know, Do: Leadership the Army Way**

The AAR has become a staple of Army procedure since it was introduced as a practice and learning tool after the Vietnam War. As defined by the Army:

"A AAR is a professional discussion of an event, focused on performance standards, that allows participants to discover from themselves what happened, why it happened, and how to sustain strengths and improve on weaknesses ... Formal AARs are scheduled after each mission and can last a few hours;

informal AARs are run consistently after other events, even if they are five minute reviews to build on lessons learned."[10]

The AAR is used in a variety of ways. It's a problem-solving mechanism; it can generate ideas for improvements; it's also a tool to socialize information across an organization. Overall, it's a fundamental organizational staple of the U.S. Army, and is used at all levels — from the platoon to the Pentagon - "to promote learning that improves performance."

The Key Elements of an AAR [11]

According to the *Army Leadership Manual*, AARs have the following characteristics. They:

✔ **Are conducted during or right after an event.** This ensures details are still fresh in the participants' minds and makes the lessons learned more immediate and compelling. For example, SEAL Team 6 performed an AAR at Bagram Air Force Base, just minutes after returning from the raid that killed Osama Bin Laden, even before they poured over the intelligence they had gathered from the compound.

✔ **Do not have areas that are off-limits for discussion**, including the leader's decisions and actions.

✔ **Involve all participants in the discussion.** Bringing in a wide variety of perspectives creates a fuller and more meaningful picture of what happened and why.

✔ **Use open-ended questions.** Discussion is not guided or shaped to reach any particular conclusion.

✔ **Determine strengths and weaknesses; looking at both provides a balanced picture.** If the discussion focuses solely on what went wrong, people aren't going to be open and honest.

✔ **Link performance to subsequent training.** The whole point of learning is to improve performance in the future.

All Army AARs follow the same general format, though they can be either formal or informal. In this case, the Army defines 'formality' by the degree of preparation and planning that go into the exercise. More casual AARs involve on-the-spot reviews of the mission, along with immediate feedback and coaching for the parties involved.

In both instances, however, the AAR generally contains the following elements:
1) Introduction
2) Review of Objectives and Intent
3) Discussion of Recent Events (What Happened)
4) Analysis of Key Issues, and
5) Concluding Summary

AARs address Weaknesses … and Strengths
Significantly, AARs are viewed as being agnostic towards success and failure; that is, they occur regardless of whether or not a mission was accomplished or not, and the process is not merely employed to catch errors. "Conducting AARs," Army leaders point out, "helps the unit ensure it does not repeat mistakes. It also helps the unit sustain strengths."

The AAR is huge part of the way in which the Army extracts intelligence from its errors, but like Toyota it cannot rely on one single procedure to institutionalize this habit. To support it, the process is underpinned by a larger set of reinforcing values. As General Anthony Zinni describes it: "we grow up in a culture where accountability, learning to accept responsibility, admitting mistakes and learning from them is critical to us."

More generally, the Army strives to "create an environment that supports people in their organizations learning from their experiences and the experiences of others. How leaders react to failure and encourage success is critical to reaching excellence. Subordinates who feel they need to hide mistakes deprive others of valuable lessons. Organizational leaders set the tone for this honest sharing of experiences by acknowledging not all experiences (even their own) are successful. They encourage subordinates to examine their experiences, and make it easy for them to share what they learn."

This is at the core of the Army's concept of leadership. Simply put, "leaders learn from their mistakes and the mistakes of others."

In fact, "there is no room for the 'zero-defects' mentality in a learning organization ... Leaders willing to learn welcome new ways of looking at things, examine what's going well, and are not afraid to look at what's going poorly ... Army leaders are taught to use those mistakes to figure out how to do things better and share what they learned with others ..."

From Military Process to Business Best Practice
The AAR is no longer a secret to others who are looking for an edge in war or simply in work. The Obama Administration regularly performs 'Look Back' exercises (their version of the AAR) when things go wrong.

Leading business guru Peter Senge, author of the bestselling book *The Fifth Discipline*, has suggested "the Army's After-Action Review is arguably one of the most successful organizational learning methods yet devised." In fact, thanks in part to Senge's promotion of the tool to his consulting clients, companies as diverse as Fed Ex, Shell and Harley Davidson have been using AARs as part of their knowledge transfer and learning architecture. As one Harley-Davidson executive put it, the AAR process "is a way to institutionalize a reflective activity. There's nothing fancy about the AAR process, but having the discipline to do it is another matter."[12]

This is a key point. The true value in the AAR process is not only in its thoroughness, but in the automaticity with which it is applied. Companies and organizations may have excellent knowledge-capture tools and frameworks in place, but if they are not used regularly, if not every time, then their usefulness diminishes considerably. One of the great insights of the U.S. Army AAR is to make its application an institutional reflex.

Centre for Army Lessons Learned
Another example of how the Army has reinforced this value is in creating an entire organization devoted to capturing the information gleaned from AARs. Named, appropriately enough, the Centre for Army Lessons Learned (CALL)[13], it collects and analyzes data from a variety of current and historical sources, including Army operations and training events, and produces lessons for military commanders, staff, and students. Established in 1985, the Centre itself is the result of a lesson learned: after the mixed success of Operation Urgent Fury, the 1984 invasion of Grenada by U.S. Forces, Army leaders called for an analysis of the engagement to better adapt group forces to local conditions. The result was a recommendation for a system to capture and disseminate lessons for the future, and CALL was born.

There is a fundamental reason why CALL's mandate is both to capture intelligence and circulate it. Learning occurs at every level of an organization in the Army's view: "someone is always experiencing something from which a lesson can be drawn." That knowledge and experience, however, must be captured and shared with others for it to have value. For this reason, the Army has put systems in place such as CALL "to collect and disseminate those lessons so that individual discoveries become organizational tools."

From Commanding Generals to Special Operators
"I learned that good judgment comes from experience, and that experience grows out of mistakes." **General Omar Bradley, U.S. Army**

David Petraeus was widely considered the greatest general of his generation until a spectacular fall from grace leading to his abrupt resignation as the Director of the Central Intelligence Agency. General Petraeus was discovered having an affair with his biographer Paula Broadwell and the resulting fallout ended his once-promising Washington career.

Long-time watchers of Petraeus might not be so ready to consider him down for the count, however; the general has made a systematic point throughout his career of learning from mistakes. In fact, his Doctoral Thesis at Princeton University was entitled "The American Military and the Lessons of Vietnam" (he listed 14 lessons learned). Petraeus' habit of plumbing the past for future wisdom was prompted by one of his mentors, General Jack Galvin, who as a younger officer had been "assigned to help write a classified history of Vietnam that became known as the Pentagon Papers. The experience gave him a behind-the-scenes look at the blunders that had led the country into a losing war." Galvin had a lot of advice for his protégé, and one was to heed the lessons of history.[14]

In no small part due to the insights he gleaned from his dissertation, Petraeus decided to take the war into a completely different direction when given command of the Iraq war in the spring of 2007. The 'surge' he implemented was more than just a tactical change, in many observers' opinions. It also "marked the end of the post-Vietnam era for the Army. Ever since that disastrous war, senior Army leaders had tried, and ultimately failed, to keep their force from becoming too deeply embroiled in messy political wars that defied standard military solutions. It was a pattern that had repeated itself in Haiti, Somalia, the Balkans, Afghanistan and then Iraq, where generals often focused more on exit strategies than on plans for victory."

It should come as no surprise that legendary generals have sought to learn from the mistakes of history. But does the soldier on the ground do likewise? They do if they're the best of the best — such as the special operators of the U.S. Army also known as Delta Force

MAGNIFICENT MISTAKES | OPERATION EAGLE CLAW

Description: Eagle Claw is the code name for the American military operation launched on April 24, 1980. President Jimmy Carter ordered troops to fly in to Iran by helicopter in an attempt to rescue the 52 Americans held hostage at the U.S. embassy. The operation stumbled right from the start, and before the commandos were able to enter Tehran's air space they experienced a combination of obstacles that forced them to abort the mission. While leaving the staging area (code named Desert One), one helicopter crashed into another aircraft, incapacitating both and killing eight servicemen aboard.

***What Went Wrong?** A series of miscalculations underscored the U.S. military did not yet have the capability to conduct this type of special operations mission. Moreover, the challenges of executing such*

a difficult operation were exacerbated by the lack of coordination between the service branches.

Lesson Learned: The Defense Department learned from this humiliating fiasco. It stood up a new command – SOCOM, or Special Operations Command – to coordinate activities between the teams that would have to collaborate in future missions. This had been one of Delta's first missions, and they studied it relentlessly for its lessons. The U.S. Air Force created a new regiment (SOAR, or Special Operations Aviation Regiment) to support future raids. Today, Delta and SOAR teams work hand in hand, conducting hundreds of missions a week together. SOCOM still exists, and its excellence is widely regarded as the reason the surge in Iraq succeeded in ending American involvement in that war. **As tragic and embarrassing as Operation Eagle Claw was, the military transformed the legacy of that loss into a magnificent mistake.** *The exceptional effectiveness of the U.S. special operations forces today can be traced back to these lessons learned.*

1st Special Forces Operational Detachment - Delta

You have probably never heard of Pete Blaber [15] or his colleagues, and the U.S. Army wants to keep that way. Blaber served as a special operator in an ultra elite organization whose name is officially classified. For 15 years, he was a member of Special Forces Operational Detachment - Delta, which has become known to the public, erroneously, as 'Delta Force'. Operators inside this exclusive group more often refer to it simply as 'The Unit,' a cryptic but fitting name for the branch of the Army dedicated to counter-terrorism and special missions.

The Unit is what the Pentagon refers to as a Tier I asset. They, along with the Naval Special Warfare Development

Group (DevGru, but also known publicly as SEAL Team 6) are considered the killer elite — the all-star team of special operators. As such, it is instructive to see how they approach the subject of failure. After all, in the world of SEALs and Delta, mistakes are more than costly: they're deadly.

Pete Blaber commanded missions in Afghanistan and was involved in the events that almost led to Osama Bin Laden's capture at Tora Bora and recounted in the book *Cobra II* by Michael Gordon and Bernard Trainor. In his own memoir describing the experience of that day and of his years inside Delta, Blaber speaks at length about the importance of drawing wisdom from the past, and especially past mistakes. In one instance, he points out: "before deploying to Afghanistan, the Unit gave each of us two books on the Soviet war in Afghanistan: the first, *The Other Side of the Mountain*, contained firsthand accounts of combat lessons from the perspective of mujahideen fighters. The second, *The Bear Went Over the Mountain*, contained firsthand accounts from the Soviet perspective."

Delta operators, Blaber explains, are taught to think creatively and make adaptive decisions. "The single most important lesson I learned … is that the most effective weapon on any battlefield … is our mind's ability to recognize life's underlying patterns. Patterns reveal how the real world works. When recognized, they allow us to understand, adapt and master the future as it unfolds in front of us."

"I believe accurately understanding and sharing lessons from the past is an essential step for gaining insight into … and preparing for the future." In this view, the past is the key to unlocking the present, and to make sound judgment calls regarding the future.

He reiterates this perspective again, when he shares the advice he received from a Vietnam veteran: "If you want to learn about what went wrong in Vietnam, you can find the answer at Gettysburg."

Like many soldiers, Blaber has a very philosophical perspective towards failure. After committing a particular egregious error, he noted he "had one more mistake to add to my lifelong résumé of mistakes, the curriculum vitae for all wisdom and knowledge." Later in his book, he states almost ruefully, "it's been said that there are no mistakes in life, only lessons. Every mistake is an opportunity to ensure that we never make it again, especially when future consequences can be much more dire."

Eric Haney is another veteran of the Unit, and he also bears witness to the fact this elite group of warriors use every opportunity to improve by learning from setbacks. In his memoir, *Inside Delta Force: The Story of America's Elite Counterterrorist Unit*, he details how "whenever we encountered a new and novel irritant on an operation, we would incorporate it into a future training session. Subsequent Operator Training Course classes caught unmitigated hell because they received the accumulated experience of every operation that preceded their arrival."[16]

Haney also describes the Unit's incredibly detailed After Action Reviews subsequent to missions. Some lasting seven hours, the postmortem's purpose "was to learn everything we possibly could about what we had just done — the good, the bad, and the ugly. We dissected problems and we came up with solutions — and the whole group profited from what we learned. There is no better way for an organization to improve itself and move forward in a professional manner."

Clearly, learning from mistakes is a staple of the U.S. Army's special operators and 4-star generals. But perhaps you think it's unique to this particular armed services branch, or even to the American military? As we're about to see, another top-flight fighting organization takes mistakes just as seriously.

CASE STUDY II - THE ISRAELI AIR FORCE (IAF)

"The Israeli Air Force is known to be one of the best in the world in part because of the time, effort and methodology that we use in briefing and debriefing. We usually start from the outcome and then we ask WHAT - WHY - HOW: What happened? Why did it happen? And finally, how can we avoid making the same mistakes and how can we improve going forward." **Amnon Shefler, Israeli Air Force Major**

Though a tiny nation of just over six million people, Israel boasts what is widely considered to be one of the world's best air forces. The IAF punches above its weight in part because its pilots are among the most battle-tested and best-trained airmen in active duty today.

It is this last point that deserves further attention. One of the key strengths of the IAF is the experience and training they provide their personnel. The former is partly a function of the fact Israel has fought in numerous 'hot' wars since its inception in 1948; the latter, however, appears to be a result of a conscious decision to invest in human as well as technological capital.

This is the distinct sense I got when I sat down with Amnon Shefler, a combat pilot with 10 years of service and one of the youngest commanders in the IAF.[17] His statements on failure are useful in illuminating how a world-class organization addresses errors. As he pointed out, "learning from mistakes is the same as learning from doing. When we act, we are going to make mistakes."

This is a theme that was reprised again and again in our conversation. The IAF is less focused on learning from mistakes than on learning from *everything* — failures, successes, and what didn't happen but could have. According to Shefler, the IAF adopts a *Kaizen* approach, and even references the concept by name: much like Toyota, they're constantly looking to improve every aspect of their training, preparation and processes. The result, as he put it, is "a system to examine what happened, to reflect on what will happen and to think deeply about how to learn from both and make the next outcome better." The IAF doesn't focus just on mistakes, of course; but they devote considerable time and energy to capturing the lessons from setbacks and defeats.

One of the chief attributes of the system they've put in place is the automaticity and immediacy with which it is implemented. "This is a habit," he said. "This is a culture. This is rooted in every pilot, but also in every support member of the IAF. It's something everyone follows. It's implemented everywhere, in every aspect of what we do. Therefore, it doesn't only happen after a mistake; it happens after every event, good or bad. It's automatic for our organization to provide that space for reflection on how we can make things better."

MAGNIFICENT MISTAKES | WHAT YOU CAN LEARN FROM ERNEST HEMINGWAY

Description: In 1940, American novelist Ernest Hemingway published For Whom The Bell Tolls, a story of an American's experience fighting in the Spanish civil war. It was an instant literary success, and it is widely regarded as his greatest novel.

What Went Wrong? *You may ask how this could be considered a mistake. The finished product is not; however, it was the culmination of many errors leading up to the final draft. Perhaps no novelist was more fastidious in his prose than Hemingway, who was famous for his terse, minimalist writing style. Legend has it that he rewrote the last page of the novel 39 times before he was satisfied. As book agent Michael Larsen points out, "that means he made 38 mistakes before getting it right." Hemingway himself put it a little more crudely: "I write one page of masterpiece to ninety pages of shit – I try to put the shit in the wastebasket."*

Lesson Learned: The practice of learning from mistakes can improve performance in every type of activity, including art.

Interestingly, the fact it happens automatically and without fail allows for the process to be that much more legitimate and accepted when it must occur after a breakdown. Indeed, the IAF strives to make the entire process professional. What makes it so is the use of a system, the lack of stigmatization of failure, and the constant effort by the organization to train its members on how to do this consistently.

"The system is taught while you're in Flight Academy," Shefler points out. As you progress through the organization, the tools you use for this system get more and more complex, detailed, and sophisticated. "We have four different kinds of tools to capture information from our flights: audio recording, video recording from the pilot and co-pilot's perspective, flight data from the plane's systems, plus data from the ground systems."

Overall, the IAF emphasizes a comprehensive and objective approach to debriefing after a mission. This also serves to de-personalize the procedure, leaving participants able to talk about errors in an objective, non-defensive way.

What | Why | How

Their process centers on asking three key questions:

What happened?

Why did it happen?

How can we do it better next time?

The beauty of the simple process is it can be enhanced by technology when possible, but it can also be implemented in its most basic form at every level of the organization, at any moment.

With regard to mission briefing, Shefler said, "we talk a lot about mistakes that have happened in the past." In fact, they actually incorporate a review of previous mistakes in the pre-mission process, right before the objective-setting phase. Then they make a point of reviewing mistakes made in prior sorties for the current mission briefing.

Three Levels of Knowledge Capture

On an individual level, every pilot keeps their own notebook or 'Lessons Learned' journal on the different missions they've had where they jot down the insights from previous errors, and those to be avoided — even when they're not the ones who made the mistake.

MAGNIFICENT MISTAKES | GARRY KASPAROV AND SNATCHING VICTORY FROM THE ASHES OF DEFEAT

Description: Garry Kasparov is a Russian grand master and is widely considered to be the world's greatest living chess player. He held the title of world champion from 1985 to 2000, when he lost his championship to his long-time nemesis Vladimir Kramnik.

What Went Wrong? *Kasparov believes in the redemptive power of loss. He is fond of quoting Simon Bolivar's observation "only an inexperienced soldier believes all is lost after being defeated for the* *first time." He didn't just talk the talk, however; after that loss in 2000, he explained how that defeat sowed the seeds for success in the rematch: "I had plenty of time to absorb exactly what Kramnik had achieved and how he had done it. I spent hours identifying and analyzing the weaknesses of mine he had exploited, and hours more figuring out how to turn the tables on Kramnik and exploit his flaws." Kasparov went on to win his rematch and regain his world number one ranking.[18]*

Lesson Learned: *Kasparov practice of systematically addressing his weaknesses shouldn't come as a surprise to even casual chess players. This philosophy is hardwired in the culture of the game, and is enshrined in the storied principle of "improving your worst piece."* **Chess, like life, is all about managing mistakes.** *Perhaps legendary grand master Savielly Tartakower put it best when he noted: "the winner of the game is the player who makes the next-to-last mistake."*

On the next level are the briefing books, which capture all of the information and lessons from the squad room as well as the IAF's doctrine about tactics, techniques and procedures. This is a more institutional repository of knowledge. Significantly, new crews rely on these briefing books until they have their own experiences upon which to draw. And since there are new teams rotating in every two years, the more experienced pilots are called upon to teach the briefing book material to the rookies, thus also re-familiarizing themselves with the lessons again in the process. It's a healthy organizational cycle that provides multiple and mutually reinforcing opportunities to learn, and be reminded of, key lessons.

Finally, there are the squad room briefings that occur before the mission. To reiterate the key themes, the squad room commander draws on his experience, as well as those of other squad room commanders and the chain of command above him, to complete the circle and provide the fullest picture possible of what is important.

Overall, the IAF knowledge capture and sharing system is intentional, comprehensive and systematic. This is probably most clearly illustrated in the emphasis they put on planning vs. flying. The ratio is startling: They typically brief for 2.5 hours for a flight that will last 20 to 45 minutes. They then de-brief for another 2.5 hours afterwards. Overall, there are 5 hours of planning and review against a maximum of 45 minutes in the air.

Why such a disparity? Shefler explains it quite simply: "the stakes are very high. Flights are dangerous, so you make the most out of every mission as an opportunity to learn."

Major Shefler has trained with a lot of other Air Forces, and he believes the IAF's processes in this regard — as well as the technology employed — is a major source of competitive advantage. The IAF is not the world's biggest air force, but it may be the best trained. The key, in Shefler's opinion, is how this approach is so deeply rooted into the culture of the organization. In fact, he has noticed how less well-trained pilots, in less modern air forces, don't have this ingrained as an institutional habit.

The IAF has "the luxury" of this time for reflection that the other branches of the Israeli Defence Forces do not, Shefler noted. If you're a tank commander, you don't have the time to pause and review a mission as carefully, in the comfort of a cockpit back at base or in a squad room. That is unique to the Air Force, and they take full advantage of this space to root the process into their culture and learning cycle. The immediacy of the opportunity to review and reflect, the vast swaths of data and intelligence gathered, and the institutional habit of doing so all combine to make this more than a just a best practice for the IAF — it makes them one of the most lethal Air Forces on Earth.

MAGNIFICENT MISTAKES | AYRTON SENNA'S LAST SECOND MONACO GRAND PRIX LOSS

Description: *Ayrton Senna was the greatest Formula One racecar driver of his generation. He won three world championships in four years between 1988 and 1991. He died while leading the 1994 San Marino (Italian) Grand Prix.*

What Went Wrong? *Senna's string of world championships began with a setback. On May 15, 1988, Senna was holding a huge lead in the Monaco Grand Prix when he crashed with less than 10 laps to go. By his own admission, he had driven recklessly in order to crush his arch rival, Alain Prost. In the documentary "Senna", he confessed that day he had "opened the window for mistakes" but he vowed to learn from them. "The mistake I made changed me psychologically and mentally," Senna said. That race was the turning point of his year, and arguably of his career: he would go on to win six of the next eight races and claim his first world championship.*

Lesson Learned: *Senna was one of the most courageous, charismatic, and ultimately tragic athletes of our time. He was James Dean, JFK and Michael Jordan all wrapped in one.* ***One of the key ways in which Senna pushed himself further and faster than anyone else of his generation was his unrelenting drive to leverage his errors.*** *As he said: "Many times it's through a mistake that you learn. And the main thing is to make sure you learn through your mistakes and get better. Making mistakes and learning from them is what made me faster."[19]*

THE LAST WORD

We've seen how top-flight organizations from fields as diverse as business and the military leverage their mistakes in a comprehensive way to gain any possible advantage against their competition. While the practices have different origins, they share a remarkable consistency in their application: they all rely on an automatic process rooted in a culture emphasizing constant improvement.

Amazon, Toyota, the U.S. Army and the Israeli Air Force all have systems in place to capture the lessons of failure. They also happen to be some of the world's leading institutions in their respective fields. Might this strategy work as well for individuals who are looking for an edge?

Absolutely. It just makes sense that we should try to learn from our mistakes. However, there is a difference between knowing what to do ... and doing what you know. The real reason both employees and executives struggle to improve their performance is because they don't know what to fix, and they don't know how to fix it. This is the challenge we turn to now — the *how*.

Chapter Two - The Speed Read

In a nutshell:
One of the best-kept secrets of truly successful people and organizations is they systematically learn from their mistakes. A formalized process is key to properly learning from mistakes. Having a well-honed routine in place is not enough: it must also be done automatically and without exception.

Points to Ponder:
- ✔ What separates Warren Buffett from other, less successful investors is not the mistakes he makes, but what he makes of them.
- ✔ the best company and organizations have carefully thought-out, established procedures for dealing with mistakes
- ✔ Toyota owes its success in no small measure to the fact that they are one of best in their industry in systematically developing the culture and capacity to learn from their mistakes.
- ✔ The U.S. Army's After Action Reviews (AARs) are supremely effective tools for capturing the lessons of failure because they occur immediately after an event, no areas are off-limits for discussion, all perspectives are considered and discussion is not guided, both strengths and weaknesses are raised, and their whole point is to improve performance in the future.
- ✔ The Israeli Air Force has a similar organizational habit that is entirely professional in nature and happens automatically and without exception. It is comprehensive and systematic while not stigmatizing error.

PUTTING IT INTO PRACTICE:

➡ Does your team or organization have a CoE or AAR it whips out each time there is a failure worth studying? If not, don't you think it should?

3

HOW:

A Second Chance at Success | How to

M.A.S.T.E.R.™ Your Mistakes

"A great nation is like a great man; when he makes a mistake, he realizes it. Having realized it, he admits it. Having admitted it, he corrects it. He considers those who point out his faults as his most benevolent teachers." **Lao Tzu**

John F. Kennedy had only been in the Oval Office for less than a hundred days when, on April 17, 1961, a small force of Cuban exiles backed by the U.S. government launched an ill-fated attack on Cuba known as the Bay of Pigs invasion. The military operation failed spectacularly in less than three days, and the dashing, glamorous young president was dealt a humiliating defeat. With his administration's credibility on the world stage in tatters after not even three months in power, Kennedy might have been sorely tempted to steer clear of foreign entanglements for the rest of his term. However, history did not cooperate, and the next fall he and the world were faced with a new Cold War flashpoint: the Cuban Missile Crisis. Would the inexperienced Commander-in-Chief falter again or rise to the occasion? "History," Mark Twain once noted, "doesn't repeat itself but it often rhymes." In this case, John F. Kennedy was able to summon an unexpected deftness and political resolve that provided a much better ending to this flashpoint for America and the world. However, the source of his newfound sagacity was, in fact, plumbed from the ashes of his earlier failure. The principal consequence of the botched Bay of Pigs operation was not, as it turns out, that an inexperienced president stumbled in the first months of his first year in office, bur rather how he responded to the mistake.[1]

First, he took full responsibility. At a State Department press conference a few days later, President Kennedy uttered one of the many phrases for which he would become famous, noting: "there's an old saying that victory has a hundred fathers and defeat is an orphan … Further statements, detailed discussions, are not to conceal responsibility because I'm the responsible officer of the Government." Second, he immediately set his most trusted advisors to the task of uncovering what went wrong.

He commissioned his brother, Attorney General Robert Kennedy, as well as General Maxwell Taylor, to analyze the mistakes the administration made in support of the Bay of Pigs invasion. The resulting report by the Cuba Study Group concluded that, among many miscues, the new president had deferred too heavily to military and intelligence officials who had been put in place during the previous Eisenhower administration. Too few assumptions they made in advocating for the invasion had been challenged and stress-tested.

As a direct consequence of both the failure at the Bay of Pigs – but also of the soul-searching that occurred after it, Kennedy changed his decision-making process. Going forward, he put in place mechanisms to ensure he'd get a wider diversity of opinions when assessing his options, while also being on guard against agenda-driven advice. Psychologist Irving Janis famously cited the Bay of Pigs fiasco as the impetus for his development of the 'groupthink' theory, which describes what can go wrong when a group of people doesn't challenge assumptions because they want to minimize conflict and conform. President Kennedy went to great lengths to avoid this trap in the future, creating the Executive Committee of the National Security Council when faced with the Cuban Missile Crisis in October 1962. Excomm, as it came to be known, was made up of a more consciously diverse set of participants than those who had advised him during the Bay of Pigs invasion.

John F. Kennedy's systematic approach to drawing the right lessons from the Bays of Pigs fiasco is an object lesson in how to learn from failure. In fact, one author entitled his 2011 book on the topic *The Brilliant Disaster*[2], echoing a notion that I have embraced with *The Magnificent Mistake.*

Most people accept that we should learn from our setbacks. But how, exactly, should that be accomplished? It's a simple question with a complex answer. This section distills the lessons of the previous chapter and synthesizes those insights into a framework I've created for how to master your mistakes. It is a six-step process captured in the acronym M.A.S.T.E.R.™:

M - **Make peace** with your mistake.

A - **Analyze** it by making a Mistake Map.

S - **Search** for the true source of the mistake by identifying the Critical Failure Factors and the Error Gene™.

T - **Take in** the right lesson (s).

E - **Eliminate** the Error Gene™ and then **Erase** the mistake.

R - **Reprogram** yourself to spot and sidestep that specific Mistake Trap™ in the future. **Repeat**.

I will also introduce a set of tools developed to support this framework, including Mistake Maps, the Error Gene™ and the Mistake Journal™.

Knowing is not the same as Doing

At this point in the book, almost everyone should agree it is a good idea to learn from your mistakes. As far as advice goes, it's right up there with "eating more vegetables" in terms of its controversiality.

There might even be a number of you who have made a point to learn from your mistakes. That only happens when we are intentional, but even those fortunate few who have the courage to examine their errors are almost certainly doing it in a haphazard, unstructured, infrequent way. Those people address miscues intuitively when they need to do it systematically.

I have discovered many of the most outstanding performers on the big stages of sport, business and even the arts consistently learn from their mistakes, and it's one of the secret ingredients to their success. We have also explored how some of the most exacting fields, from fighting wars to flying planes, depend on this practice to make these high-risk activities more safe and successful.

That we need to learn from mistakes is common sense. Knowing how to do so, however, is an uncommon virtue. It is precisely that point — the how — on which we will focus our attention now.

I've distilled the principles behind the Magnificent Mistake™ process by studying the winners across a variety of fields. The M.A.S.T.E.R.™ Checklist is as much a product of Thomas Edison, Ted Williams and Toyota as it is from my reflections on error. But I've also leveraged the best practices we have uncovered in business and the military. As a result, the M.A.S.T.E.R.™ Framework combines market and battle-tested principles, checklists as well as proven forensic practices.

The choice of the acronym is quite deliberate: to "master" something is to conquer or overcome. This process will empower you to overcome the legacy of your errors. One can never truly erase a mistake, but through this method we can change their longer-term consequences, as well as ensure our miscues don't come to define us.

This multiphase approach is a practical, rather than theoretical, one. Learning from the science of checklists, I took to heart the advice that any such tool must be simple to remember, easy to use, and quick to implement. As well, the framework also builds on the well-known importance of — and reliance on — habits, checklists, systems and processes.

It isn't just a cute mnemonic device, either. First, this is a strategy and a system for learning from your mistakes. The checklist sets out the important elements of a successful strategy so that you cover each step, in sequence.

Second, it's also both a lesson and a recipe: a lesson on how to learn from error quickly and systematically, and a recipe for how to repeat it over and over. The M.A.S.T.E.R.™ Checklist represents a carefully crafted, comprehensive and stress-tested approach to making the most of your mistakes.

Now that I've explained the rationale behind the process, let's get started.

Step 1: MAKE PEACE with your Mistake
"Confession of errors is like a broom which sweeps away the dirt and leaves the surface brighter and clearer. I feel stronger for confession."
Mahatma Gandhi

I spent four years working as a Press Secretary on Capitol Hill, and there is a saying in Washington, DC that one should always "get out in front of bad news."

Simply put, you need to own your mistakes, admit to them early on in the process, and most importantly take responsibility for them. Trying to hide them is the worst strategy, as the cover-up is often worse than the crime (see the Watergate saga for proof).

This advice, however sound, is not one often followed in those corridors of power. Given the nature of politicians' antagonistic relationship with the press, Capitol Hill culture creates an environment that actually encourages burying mistakes rather than broadcasting them. Did you ever wonder why bad news always seems to come out of Washington on Fridays for example? Savvy communications directors know that this is the best day of the week to 'drop' information you'd just as soon not make the headlines — and a long holiday weekend is even better. The thinking behind this 'Friday strategy' is that people might overlook little news nuggets more as they turn their attention to the weekend.

All of these efforts to dim the spotlight on errors are understandable to some degree. Most people refuse to even look at why things went wrong, and there are powerful psychological forces at play in that reluctance. "Research suggests strong emotions often prompt people to blame others or external events rather than themselves so that they can maintain some semblance of self-esteem and a sense of control." People don't take responsibility for their actions because they will be forced to accept their fallibility. It's easier to shift blame than accept the inconvenient truth we're not perfect.

But this is not the only reason we act this way. Another mental hurdle we struggle to overcome is found in the principle of loss aversion. In simple terms, we hate losing more than we love winning. This is why mistakes sting so much. Think back to a time when you lost something important — a hockey game, a job, a friendship or girlfriend. Now recall an instance when you got what you wanted; chances are that the pain of the loss is more vivid and more powerful. When our ancestors spent their days out on the Savannah, being chased by lions, the consequences of 'getting it wrong' were so deadly evolution has hardwired us to fear setbacks far more than we covet successes. Part of the challenge in owning our mistakes is in overcoming that particular genetic inheritance.

Despite these psychological tendencies, it's clear that we can't begin to learn from our mistakes until we first admit we have made them. Confronting our errors isn't easy, and it often hurts. People want to skip over this step, but nothing can happen until they do. Facing your mistakes is not about wasting energy on regrets, or beating up on yourself. It's about identifying the 'own goals' sabotaging your performance and then focusing on what you need to improve.

Think about it as problem solving, not fixing character flaws. Context is everything; if you change the framework of thinking about an error, it loses its power to paralyze. It's a subtle but powerful shift allowing people to look at their false steps without personalizing them, or making judgments on their ability or character. When accepting your mistakes, forget about blame and concentrate on modifiability.

It's critical to overcome the paralysis of regret that often accompanies a major mistake. We've all felt the fear that we won't be able to overcome a significant error, or its potentially long-lasting consequences. In times like these, I find guidance in a wise and comforting Chinese proverb: "the best time to have planted a tree was 25 years ago. But the second-best time is today." Whether we realize it or not, almost every mistake's legacy can be changed; the key is to start the process right away.

We don't usually do this because people regularly overestimate the cost of admitting an error; the irrational fear of facing that mistake often outweighs the actual consequences of doing so. The perceived psychological 'price' they expect to pay is almost always exaggerated, but it's that fear that paralyzes people into avoiding reality.

For all of these reasons, people tend to bury their miscues when in fact we should do the exact opposite. Perhaps you believe it's unrealistic to think we can be honest about making mistakes, especially in the 'real' world of your professional life. Tell that to A.G. Lafley, the legendary CEO of Procter & Gamble, who has made a career of speaking out about his stumbles. "In his book *The Game-Changer*, he lists and even celebrates his 11 most expensive product failures, focusing on what the company learned from each."[3]

Lafley is not the only senior executive who is famous for his openness about his errors. Richard Branson has openly embraced making mistakes, passing along the following advice: "do not be embarrassed by your failures. Learn from them and start again."

If they can do it, why can't you? You can — and here's how.

Face > Own > Embrace

So one has to admit a mistake before being able to go any further in the process. This is the first, perhaps most important, and certainly the hardest step. Before we can examine our defeats in depth, we have to face our flaws.

We can't just admit our errors: we also have to own them. This means accepting the mistake, and the responsibility of its consequences. Only after having vanquished these two psychological hurdles can we come to embrace the setback.

Let's return, for a moment, to the time when I was a congressional press secretary, and the occasion of my first serious professional blunder. I managed to secure one of the best jobs in Washington, DC – and almost lost it in my first week in the position.

I had just started serving as the spokesperson for a congressman from California, and he had left town to go back to the district (in this case, San Diego) with the chief of staff. I fielded a phone call from a journalist from our local newspaper inquiring about a military base in the district that was potentially slated for closure, and for a comment from the congressman. Before he and the chief of staff had left, they had given me a thorough briefing on all of the likely issues of the week — and this hadn't been one of them. I quickly rifled through my notes while talking to the journalist, and then, seeing no mention of the base closure on any of the talking points, simply responded to him with what I thought was a non-committal answer: "it's not on our radar screen at the moment." He thanked me for my quick reply, and we both went about our day.

The next morning, all hell broke loose. The headline of the local paper screamed: *Congressman's aide says base closure "not on our radar screen."* The phone immediately started ringing, and it was the big boss. He was not pleased — at all. After giving me a number of choice words to describe my work, he hung up in utter disgust.

I was pretty sure I was done as his press secretary. Not even a week on the job and I might be headed out the door before the seat even got warm. The chief of staff was calmer about the situation, and pointed out to the congressman they had not briefed me on some secret negotiations that had been undertaken in order to stave off the base closure. They had not told me … but I had not bothered to think before inserting my foot in my mouth with my glib comment. There were two mistakes made, but mine was by far the bigger one.

I resolved in that moment to tackle the error head on. The congressman was due back in the office later that afternoon, and I booked in 15 minutes with him as soon as he had a free moment. I walked in to his office, apologized profusely for the error, took full responsibility for the mistake, and told him that I understood completely if he felt the need to terminate my employment. I didn't equivocate on my role in the blunder, or offer explanations as to why it was an honest mistake. I owned up to being responsible for it and accepted the reality that this could be a firing offense. Thankfully, the congressman didn't, and I went on to successfully work for him for another 18 months without any major missteps. Later, he would tell me that it was that instance of taking full responsibility that convinced him I was going to serve him well. I was going to make missteps, and the important thing, for him, was how quickly I would learn from them. With that lapse in judgment seared in my mind, I never responded to a journalist's unexpected question with an off-the-cuff answer again. Faced with the same trap a few weeks later, in fact, I politely told the journalist I'd have to get back to him and promptly did so, *after* checking with the chief of staff and the congressman first.

I share this personal anecdote for a few reasons: first, to underscore we all mess up. Second, I experienced the power of facing and owning up to an error first hand, and can attest it's the only way to deal with a misstep. Finally, embracing the mistake allowed me to learn a lesson from it, which in turn helped me become a better employee. So when I advocate this sequence for Step 1 of the M.A.S.T.E.R.™ Framework, I speak as someone who has lived to tell the tale of a potentially disastrous screw-up.

Summary
These three preliminary steps — facing, owning and embracing — are critical to surviving the initial moments after a mistake, and they prepare us for the next stage in the process: figuring out what went wrong. Only by admitting that we made a mistake can we make that error a part of our past; only by learning from it can we leverage it into wisdom for the future.

STEP 2: ANALYZE YOUR MISTAKE

It's not enough to take responsibility for your missteps. While this is necessary, it's not sufficient to transform the error into a source of wisdom going forward. For that, you need to tease out the reasons for the mistake.

The M.A.S.T.E.R.™ Approach requires you to be willing to examine yourself with unflinching honesty and uncommon rigor. In medical terms, we will perform a forensic analysis of your mistake. To use a transportation analogy, at this stage we want to open up the 'black box' of your error.

But how best to do that? This is where we rely on the fields from which those two metaphors came, and leverage the best practices from those and other disciplines to be as meticulous and comprehensive as possible.

First, we need to remind ourselves what we were trying to accomplish. Then we'll analyze the sequence of events that led to the error. Finally, we will properly define the problem inasmuch detail as is needed. We do so by first asking the 2 Whats and the 5 Whys.

The 2 Whats

It may seem obvious, but any investigation should start with a reminder of the facts as we know them. For this, we use the 2 Whats:

What did we set out to do? (Objective)

What actually happened? (Outcome)

In an autopsy, it could be as simple as: a man was alive, and now he's dead. In an airplane crash, we might say that the objective was for Flight 007 to take off in New York and land safely in London 5 hours later. The outcome, unfortunately, was it crashed shortly after getting aloft.

The purpose of this step is to put the key facts front and center. Too often, we fail to properly frame an investigation at the outset. As a result we run the risk of going off-course right away. This step focuses the mind and the subsequent line of inquiry on a specific target.

Finding the Tripping Point

The critical question at this juncture is: What Went Wrong? In some sense, this is the line of investigation we pursue to understand what happened between the 2 Whats: the desired objective and the actual outcome. It's less of an exhaustive examination (that will come later) as the identification and definition of the turning point where the objective went off the rails. Knowing where, exactly, defeat was snatched from the jaws of victory will help us know where to focus our analytical gaze.

The key is to ignore all of the distracting clues to isolate and identify the core of the issue. The Japanese have a useful concept to crystallize this point. The *genba* is the term they use for the heart of an operation, problem or situation. As Chip and Dan Heath point out in their book *Decisive*, *genba* means "the real place or, more loosely, the place where the action happens. Japanese detectives, for instance, call the crime scene the *genba*. In a manufacturing firm, the *genba* would be the factory floor, and for a retailing company it would be the store."[4] As they advise, when assessing your assumptions before making a decision, we should do the same to analyze our mistakes: go to the *genba* to understand problems.

The 5 Whys

The final step is to drill down into the details of the event. We turn to a handy tool borrowed from engineering called the 5

Whys (which we discovered with Toyota in the previous chapter). The idea, you'll recall, is to keep asking 'Why' five times (or more) until you have identified the root causes of the mistake. The key is to trace your error to its source: where, exactly, did we go wrong? For that, one needs to use the following tools and tips.

You want to start by making a Mistake Map as a diagnostic tool. This consists of drawing a Decision Tree going back up the branch of the mistake. Where did the critical fault line occur? You want to brainstorm in this phase and capture and collect all possible sources of the mistake before determining which is the actual cause.

It's critical you use the right time horizons and appropriately limit the frame of analysis. Unless you have the correct period for evaluating performance, you are likely to misconstrue the factors that led to success or failure. It's much easier to establish cause and effect when actions and outcomes are close together in time.

Finally, one way to create a positive environment while still answering these rhetorical questions is to use the process to identify the good and the bad. As we discovered in the last chapter, the U.S. Army emphasizes this in their after-action reviews in order to ensure they look at both to provide a balanced picture. If the discussion focuses solely on what went wrong, people aren't going to be open and honest. Also, don't close your mind to anything: Patterns can be meaningful, but so can anomalies. Pay attention to both in order to get the fullest picture of what might have gone wrong.

Summary
Step 2 is all about using key frameworks and diagnostic tools to dispassionately examine your mistake. By looking at it from

50,000 feet (the 2 Whats), 5 feet (going to the *genba*) and 5 inches (the 5 Whys), you can grasp every possible angle of the event. It's this critical investigation that makes the next step possible.

STEP 3: SEARCH FOR THE TRUE SOURCE OF THE MISTAKE

If the previous stage was all about analyzing your error, this one is focused on understanding your mistake. Specifically, you need to ensure you are learning the right lessons from this breakdown.

When I suggest we have to understand our miscue, I really only mean we unpack them to the extent we can side-step the trigger or foresee its repeat before it happens. Just as we don't need to know hydrodynamics is involved when we slip in the rain to stop it from happening, we don't need to know the inner recesses as to why. A good way to think about the threshold of knowledge needed is to follow this principle: "If you can't explain the reason, you don't know the reason."

When assessing the reasons for error, it's critical to forget about blame and concentrate on modifiability — what you can actually change in your behavior to avoid a repeat of that mistake in the future. You begin by finding the Critical Failure Factors (CFFs), and figuring out what the Compound Consequences (CCs) of your mistake are, so you can ultimately fix the right problems.

What is a Critical Failure Factor? They are the key decisions, moments or events where things began to go wrong. They represent the opposite of its significantly better-known cousin, the Critical Success Factor. Another way of describing them is as the 'strategic inflection points' (a term popularized by Andy Grove of Intel) leading to the mistake, defeat or collapse.

This is easier than it sounds. There is rarely a single 'point of failure,' to borrow a concept from Information Technology architecture; rather, there are often 'mistake chains'. Indeed, in many disasters, the chain of causation is intricate. This is where the Mistake Map that you draw will come in handy. It will pinpoint the sequence of events that led to the error.

Determining the Compound Consequences

You then want to project forward and identify what I call the Compound Consequences (CCs) of your mistake: these are the second and third order effects of your decisions. The CCs can be found in the downstream impact of a decision (or series of decisions) that have combined and grown quickly (like compound interest) to create a particularly negative situation. You have captured the full extent of the error's impact this way. By doing so, you will reduce the possibility related mistakes are treated separately. It's critical to grasp all of the ramifications of the initial error.

The most important principle to remember about this stage is to beware of "reading history wrong." You want to ensure you are identifying the correct things to correct. At the same time, one should also be on the lookout for patterns in your errors. There is a repetitive element to almost every mistake. One caveat, however; there is a risk that instead of discovering a pattern you "generate" one — much like a doctor sometimes misdiagnoses a patient by leading a patient through a series of questions designed to confirm (rather than elicit) certain assumptions. Be mindful of the common problem in psychology known as the confirmation bias, namely a tendency of people to process information in a way that confirms their beliefs or how it fits an existing narrative about a situation.

Summary
Once we've catalogued all of the important details surrounding the mistake, we will finally be able to achieve the principal objective of the whole process: absorb the wisdom in this wake-up call.

STEP 4: TAKE IN THE KEY LESSON (S)

The 4 Cs and the 3 Is
It seems obvious, but the whole point of learning something is to improve performance in the future. The hard-earned knowledge you've just extracted from your mistake will only be useful if you do something with it. So you have to capture, crystallize, commit and communicate (4 Cs) what you've learned.

Capturing the lesson is memorializing the specific cause and effect relationship ("I crashed when I took my eyes off the road to return a txt message.")

Then you have to distill the take-away into the most succinct prescriptive formulation possible by crystallizing it down to its essence ("Don't txt and drive. Period.")

You subsequently commit to the direction in a clear expression of resolve ("I will never txt while driving.")

Finally, communicate this new rule where and when necessary ("I swear to you, Mom, I will never txt again while driving.")

There are a few other steps if you are addressing an error that has affected others, or that should be shared across an organization. In this case, you must incorporate and institutionalize the lessons learned immediately (3 Is).

This is critical, as author and doctor Atul Gewande points out:

> "Sometimes ... when failures are investigated. We learn better ways of doing things. And then what happens? Well, the findings might turn up in a course or seminar, or they might make it into a professional journal or a textbook. In ideal circumstances, we issue some inch-thick set of guidelines ... But incorporating the changes often takes years."[5]

If you are successful in completely absorbing the lesson it will come to you reflexively, without conscious effort at recollection. In a sense, you are using this learning process to educate your intuition. "Garry Kasparov, the chess grand master, obsessively studied his past matches, looking for the slightest imperfection, but when it came time to play a chess game, he said he played by instinct, 'by smell, by feel.' "[6]

Summary
Capture, crystallize, codify and communicate (4Cs) what you've learned. If you're in an organization, incorporate and institutionalize those lessons immediately (3Is).

STEP 5: ELIMINATE THE ERROR GENE™ AND ERASE THE MISTAKE
Once you have identified the right problem, all that remains is focusing on what you have to change. This is why you have

to eliminate what I have coined the Error Gene™. I use the language of genetics purposely; a gene is the smallest, most irreducible source of hereditary traits in a human being.

Accordingly, I want you to drill down to the most molecular level when you're attacking the source of your mistake. In a sense, we're performing gene therapy, only the defect is not biological but behavioral.

One practical consequence of this focus is one becomes mindful not to correct the symptom, rather than the cause, of the mistake. To extend the medical analogy, we want to treat the gene like a cancerous one; therefore, we should attempt to remove only the malignant part of the behavior pattern causing the mistake. Using the basic example we sketched out above, there is no reason to stop driving entirely when all that is required is to stop texting and driving.

Both parts of this stage are crucial. It's just as important to erase the mistake once you've successfully eliminated what caused it. You learn from the past, but you shouldn't live in it.

Summary
This step can be summed up simply: remember the lesson; forget the mistake.

STEP 6: REPROGRAM YOURSELF TO SPOT AND SIDESTEP THIS MISTAKE IN THE FUTURE. REPEAT THIS PROCESS (OVER AND OVER)
The final action is arguably the most critical to making this a long-term best practice. Essentially, you train your brain to develop an early warning system for mistakes.

Part of the challenge of anticipating repeat errors is to be on the lookout for Mistake Traps™ you routinely commit.

Armed with your new knowledge, ask yourself: what mistakes do I usually make in this instance?

The 'R' in M.A.S.T.E.R.™ could just as easily stand for 'Recognize,' as in spotting the tripwire to your usual error. The reprogramming will be successful when a little alarm bell goes off in your head before you make that familiar mistake.

Once you are alerted and attuned to your error patterns, you'll begin see them everywhere. The key to this process is first analysis and then recognition. Once you've primed yourself, your unconscious brain will start scanning the environment appropriately. After some practice, the process won't have to be conscious at all; it will be automatic.

In this way, you begin to reprogram yourself. Whereas you used to be susceptible to certain types of behaviors, the process we've just outlined allows you to identify these trouble spots ahead of time. Once you recognize a destructive pattern, it becomes much easier to avoid it going forward.

Finally, it's critical to 'encode' the lessons of your previous mistakes — ideally, by identifying the trigger(s) and preparing a preventative checklist. Embedded behaviors cause us to repeat mistakes are like biases. Unfortunately, as psychologists point out, we can't deactivate our biases, but we can counteract them with the right discipline. That discipline is the M.A.S.T.E.R.™ Checklist.

This whole approach will take time to sink in, but its application only gets easier the more often you use it. The ultimate goal is you come to apply it repeatedly and reflexively. Learning from even one chronic mistake will make you better, to be sure; learning to leverage many, if not all of your errors over time will make you the best you can be. Going forward, this process should become one of your high-performance habits.

THE LAST WORD
"The system is the solution." **Slogan at AT&T**

The M.A.S.T.E.R.™ Checklist is a practical tool for how to quickly draw the lessons from your error and turn it into a Magnificent Mistake™. It's a framework that can be applied to the full spectrum of screw-ups we commit every day — the personal ones as well as the professional ones. It is simple enough to remember easily and do on the spot; nimble enough to apply to big mistakes as well as small blunders; and comprehensive enough to make sure you are capturing the right lessons and incorporating them into future decisions.

The Checklist should be used formally and in great detail or very quickly, after a little near miss or small mistake. That's why it's a checklist and a mnemonic: to make it easy for you to whip out and apply it in day-to-day decisions as well as more elaborate look-back reviews or investigations. It's equally adept and applicable at the micro-level as at the macro-level. It's important to go through the 6 steps sequentially, but you can do it 'quick and dirty' if necessary. But having a strict formula is not really the point. The magic is not in the complexity of the task; the magic is in the doing of simple things repeatedly.

THE M.A.S.T.E.R.™ CHECKLIST'S INTELLECTUAL INSPIRATIONS
I developed this tool in part by studying the way top individuals and organizations address their mistakes. I also took inspiration from the best practices I've discovered and distilled in my research — from making information 'sticky' to the process by which we build and sustain habits.

*The idea to capture the steps of the process in a **memorable mnemonic and acronym** was inspired by Chip and Dan Heath's book, Made to Stick. In it, they argue persuasively if a lesson is easy to remember, it will be more likely to be applied.*

*Turning this framework into a **checklist** was a consequence of reading Atul Gewande's excellent tome on the power of such devices, The Checklist Manifesto.*

*The importance of turning these steps into behaviors, then **habits**, became clear after reading Charles Duhigg's The Power of Habits (and by brushing up on Aristotle, who famously said: "We are what we repeatedly do. Excellence, therefore, is not an act but a habit.")*

*Finally, it was after observing Amazon and Toyota's systematic approach to mistakes, as well as observing David Allen's equally methodical approach to To-Do Lists through his GTD (Getting Things Done) process, that I realized that any mistake management tool had to be a comprehensive **system**.*

This framework should transform the way you look at mistakes. Now you do not have to fear making errors, or resist acknowledging them. In fact, we should not have a 'zero tolerance' approach towards false steps. Messing up is natural, unavoidable, and even desirable in some cases. The Nobel Laureate in Physics, Frank Wilczek once pointed out, "If you're not making enough mistakes, you're not working on hard enough problems. And that's a mistake."

We shouldn't tolerate making the same errors over and over, however, our intolerance shouldn't be applied to the first mistake, but *to the second*. On the contrary, the first one is valuable. The second is not. There are serious diminishing marginal returns to mistakes.

This process is all about making constant, but small, course corrections. If you do so, you will follow what Pentagon thinker Thomas Barnett calls a 'spiral development' process: "Improvements are achieved in an iterative fashion, allowing for adaptation over time to changes."[7]

Indeed, you will get better at this each time you do it. Transforming mere errors into magnificent mistakes is a trainable skill. But it's not one that we develop naturally. We have an inherent bias towards looking through the windshield, rather than the rear view mirror, in thinking about life — yet that's also a big mistake, in some ways. It is one Nathan Myhrvold, the former CTO of Microsoft, knows to be true. "Everyone thinks the past is uninteresting," he says. "It's not hot. It's not new. I love the idea of the future, but the future isn't here yet. If you want to make good decisions about what's to come, look behind you."

We began this chapter with an anecdote about how President John F. Kennedy learned from the Bay of Pigs failure to spot flaws in his foreign policy decision-making process. It turns out that JFK learned from history as much as from experience: biographers have reported that, somewhat fortuitously, immediately prior to the Cuban Missile Crisis he had just read Barbara Tuchman's Pulitzer-prize-winning book *The Guns of August*.[8] Tuchman's historical tome details how a small, seemingly insignificant act — the assassination of the Archduke Franz Ferdinand, heir apparent to the throne of the Austro-Hungarian empire — set in motion a series of events that led to World War I. It appears that President Kennedy had the missteps of what transpired earlier that century in mind when considering how close to the brink he could go in his confrontation with Russia that fall.

In the next section of the book, we will learn how to apply this notion of learning from history and experience in practical ways, and in particular how they can be applied in the context of our everyday lives.

CHAPTER THREE - THE SPEED READ

IN A NUTSHELL:

Transforming mere errors into magnificent mistakes is a trainable skill, but it's not one we do naturally. We have to follow a process to make constant but small course corrections. The M.A.S.T.E.R.™ Checklist provides a framework and a checklist to quickly, comprehensively and systematically learn from your mistakes.

POINTS TO PONDER:

✔ Admit your mistake.
✔ Face and then own your error.
✔ Capture and collect all possible sources of the mistake.
✔ Identify the good as well as the bad.
✔ Understand your mistake completely.
✔ Ensure that you are identifying the correct things to correct.
✔ Be on the lookout for patterns in your errors.
✔ The hard-earned knowledge you've just extracted will only be useful if you do something with it. So you have to capture, crystallize, codify and communicate what you've learned.
✔ There are a few other steps if you are addressing an error that has affected others, or that should be shared across an organization. In this case, you must incorporate and institutionalize the lessons learned immediately.
✔ You are using this learning process to educate your intuition.

✔ Remember the lesson. Forget the mistake.

✔ Reprogram yourself to avoid that Mistake Trap™ going forward.

✔ This approach will take time to master, but its application only gets easier the more often you use it. The ultimate goal is you come to apply it repeatedly and reflexively.

PUTTING IT INTO PRACTICE:

➡ Think about a mistake you've made recently. How did you react? Did you try to shift blame, or explain it away — or did you face, own and embrace its consequences?

➡ Draw up a Mistake Map of the error, trying to pinpoint exactly where the critical misstep occurred.

➡ Identify the full extent of the error's impact *and* determine the Compound Consequences.

4

NOW:

THE 12 MAGNIFICENT MISTAKE HABITS™ PUTTING THIS PHILOSOPHY INTO PRACTICE IN YOUR LIFE AND ORGANIZATION

"99% of my life is failures, because we're building prototypes all the time. We're trying out ideas, and they all fail. You then have to try and make it work, and that requires hundreds or thousands of prototypes — all of which are failures — until you get the one success. So we're totally used to failure. Failure is fascinating. It's much more interesting than success." **James Dyson, Inventor and CEO of Dyson Electronics**

What do you do to pass the time when you're an elite commando deployed on a secret mission in Asia? Why, come up with an idea that became a $50 million company, of course.[1]

That's exactly what Randy Hetrick did back in 1997, when, frustrated at the lack of options he had to stay in peak shape while out in the field, the Navy SEAL commander jury-rigged a harness he used to perform a variety of modified body weight exercises. He and his fellow special operators came to use the invention — which they unceremoniously called 'the gizmo' — extensively while on deployments, but no one in their wildest dreams suspected it might become an outright fitness sensation a few decades later. Today, the system of straps Hetrick devised is now known as TRX (Total-Body-Resistance Exercise), and the company behind it has over 100 employees and generates in excess of $50 million in annual revenue.

What is the secret to TRX's success? Those who use the system laud its portability, as evidenced by the product's catchy slogan: "Make Your Body Your Machine." Hetrick was also shrewd in building word of mouth for the suspension training system, leveraging the celebrity of all things Navy SEAL but also targeting professional athletes and trainers in gyms. Perhaps most important of all, though, he constantly tweaked and refined his product, incorporating feedback from fellow SEALs and early adopter athletes. By his own count, Hetrick fiddled with his design over 50 times before arriving at the finished product that fills gym floors and hotel rooms today. Put another way, he made 49 or so mistakes along the way, but used those failures to eliminate the non-essential and improve the 'gizmo' every step of the way. In so doing, Hetrick displayed a number of key behaviors — counter-intuitive to some, but ultimately ultra-productive in perfecting his product — that certainly contributed to his longer-term success.

As we have learned, you can generate a wealth of wisdom from your mistakes. While the benefits to your personal life are obvious, applying this principle in your professional activities as well can yield even larger-scale improvements. The creator of the TRX system can testify to that, and in the coming pages we will learn some specific practices to bring this philosophy to life.

Mostly everyone has heard of Stephen Covey's *7 Habits for Highly Effective People*. Emulating that spirit, I'd like to suggest 12 Magnificent Mistake Habits™ you should install in your own career or organization. Each one reinforces the truth we have discovered, namely that focusing on failure is actually the fastest route to success. The 12 Habits are a set of closely related concepts and behaviors designed to increase the likelihood that you're making the most of every mistake. Collectively, they will make you and your team more accountable, more innovative, and more effective. Let's get started.

MM Habit 1: Don't fear errors and resist waiting for a 'perfect' moment: apply the 70% rule

Many organizations find themselves frozen in place at some point because they don't want to make a misstep. If only we wait a little longer, they say, we'll have enough information to make the right decision. This is often described as 'paralysis by analysis.'

The Marine Corps don't have that luxury. Time and space for reflection are not often found in combat or wartime conditions. This is why as an organization they focus on getting just the right amount of information they need before mobilizing. This bias for action is especially prevalent in the planning stage of an operation, and the formula they follow is simple: if you have 70% of the data, have done 70% of the analysis, and feel 70% confident, then make your move.[2]

For the Marines, the decision point comes after crossing a threshold of optimal information; they choose to optimize rather than maximize their preparations before engaging.

They realize a less than ideal action, swiftly executed, stands some chance of success, while the worst move is to make no decision at all.

All organizations have to be decisive in order to succeed, and part of that power comes from having the confidence to act. So don't be paralyzed by the fear of mistakes; have a bias for action like the Marines, and don't wait for a 'perfect' moment. As the Chinese say, "avoid defeat and you will avoid success."

MM HABIT 2 : FOCUS ON GETTING BETTER RATHER THAN BEING GOOD

Once you've taught yourself and the members of your organization or team to ignore the quest for 'perfection,' it's important to reframe how they come to regard the mistakes they are sure to make. The key is to communicate the end goal is improvement, not excellence.

Why is this so critical? Quite simply, everybody can improve ... but not everyone can be excellent. The goal of "getting better" is achievable and, therefore, motivating. Being good — or getting great — may come in time, but as an objective it can seem out of reach.

Give your team permission to screw up. "Studies show when people feel they are allowed to make mistakes, they are significantly less likely to actually make them." By doing so, you take the anxiety out of the situation, which is the principal driver for errors in the first place.

Demanding perfection is also a counter-productive objective when we know that, even if it were attainable, it cannot be without incremental improvements along the way. Computer coders live by this credo when they release betas of their programs or applications, preferring to 'launch and learn' rather than wait for a perfect product. Similarly, the Lean Start-Up movement follows the same principle: they commit to an iterative process where the business model and products are subjected almost immediately to the critical eye of the marketplace. They understand that there is value in launching your next idea before you think it's ready. The animated film studio Pixar follows this same principle, and in the colorful language of one of their executives you see it in action: Co-founder and President Ed Catmull describes their creative process as "going from suck to non-suck." Another of their top leaders expresses their approach less memorably, but perhaps even more profoundly: "we don't actually finish our films, we release them."[3]

One of my favorite maxims is "don't let the perfect be the enemy of the good." Apply this principle to your career, your family or your team, and watch how your attitude changes towards the setbacks you will encounter along the way. Believe it or not, sometimes good is good enough.

MM HABIT 3: STUDY YOUR SUCCESSES THIS WAY, TOO

The M.A.S.T.E.R.™ Checklist can become a decision-making tool to help you look forward, too. Don't wait for mistakes to put the approach into practice; in fact, you should not apply it solely to errors. The analytical rigor the checklist provides can also be turned to study successes in the same way.

I learned this lesson from a nineteenth century English poet. Rudyard Kipling is famous to millions of children for having written *The Jungle Book*. He's perhaps best known to adults for his masterful poem about the passage to manhood, 'If'. In it, Kipling addresses, albeit obliquely, the false idols of success and failure when he writes in this elegiac couplet [4]:

> *If you can meet with triumph and disaster*
> *And treat those two impostors just the same*

I have taken a great deal of solace from Kipling's advice over the years. As I said at the outset, part of my motivation for writing a book about mistakes is I've made a lot of them myself. Treating 'disaster like an impostor' has proven to be a great remedy in tough times, and is the philosophical starting point for the ideas underpinning this book. But just as I've come to learn failure can, if well understood, be fleeting, so too can success.

Look at the falls from grace by the likes of once titanic companies such as BlackBerry; what we see is that success is temporary, and therefore so is failure. What matters most is building resilience from setbacks, as well as reflecting on the true causes of either state, because it is likely to change soon anyway.

A lot of top organizations have come to treat success and failure in a similarly skeptical manner. The world's most successful animated movie studio Pixar, for instance, "conducts rigorous reviews of the process used to make each of its films — regardless of whether they're hits or misses."

"Virtually all leaders recognize the need to learn from failures, but amazingly few try to understand the true causes of their firms' successes." The bottom line is you should study success as systematically as we trained ourselves to examine failure. You'll be surprised at what you'll learn about what actually contributed to your success.

In fact, the same steps that form the basis for the M.A.S.T.E.R.™ Checklist can be applied to systematically analyze your triumphs:

Step 1: MAKE PEACE with your ~~Mistake~~ Success > Get over yourself. It probably had as much to do with luck as what you did.

Step 2: ANALYZE your ~~Mistake~~ Success > Use the same tools.

Step 3: SEARCH for the Right Lesson > Identify the specific reason for your success.

Step 4: TAKE IN the Lesson > Incorporate that insight into future thinking.

Step 5: ~~ELIMINATE the Error Gene~~™ **and ERASE the ~~mistake~~ success** > Do not bask in your victories. The glow should fade quickly so you can get back to working towards the next one.

Step 6: ~~REPROGRAM yourself to spot and sidestep this mistake in the Future.~~ REPEAT this process.

So the next time you've experienced a stunning success, remember theses words of wisdom from English novelist George Eliot "there are many victories worse than defeat."

MM HABIT 4: MAKE THE MOST OF YOUR NEAR MISSES

This is a book about mistakes, though, and the bulk of our attention should still be turned to the miscues we make. As we've already seen, the M.A.S.T.E.R.™ Checklist is a useful tool to do so. But can it be applied to every type of mistake?

It might shock you to hear this, but it may be even more important to apply this principle to small errors rather than big ones. Sometimes you can avoid huge mistakes in the future by making the most of your 'near misses.'

The idea that we should pay attention to these close calls comes from a provocative *Harvard Business Review* article, "Preventing catastrophe by learning from near-misses" by Peter M. Madsen.[5] In it, the author points out teams and organizations often fail to expose and correct latent errors that surface in near misses. Thus, missing an opportunity to

improve even when the cost of doing it is small and not correcting it might lead to a disaster in the future.

First, let's be clear about what we mean by the term 'near
misses.' As defined by the article's author, they are "successful outcomes in which luck played a key role in averting
disaster." To this articulation I would add another variant,
namely unremarkable, small missteps. We often ignore, at
our peril, the little mistakes we make along the way when
they don't produce disastrous outcomes. Spilling coffee on
a freshly ironed dress shirt or blouse is not a true calamity,
so we usually chalk up the error to inattention or rushing
out the door. But behind that inconsequential accident probably is a more fundamental shortcoming, which is you didn't
set aside enough time to prepare your departure from the
house that morning. It is that mistake — the lack of proper
planning — which might prove to be costly in the future if
you allow the near miss you just experienced to go unnoticed
and unstudied.

Why is it so important to analyze close calls? Because they
almost always presage major mistakes. Near misses are the leading indicators of imminent failure. "Organizational disasters,
studies show, rarely have a single cause … Rather, they are ini-
tiated by the unexpected interaction of multiple small, often
seemingly unimportant, human errors, technological failures,
or bad business decisions. These latent errors combine with enabling conditions to produce a significant failure."

The authors emphasize two important elements that are
present in catastrophic failures: 'latent errors' and 'enabling
conditions.' While these come to light in disasters, they are
also revealed in close calls; however we simply don't pay
enough attention to them. This is the systematic mistake we

all make in laughing off our near misses: rather than experiencing relief, we should plunge into reflection about what might have happened, and why.

They offer particularly useful opportunities to draw out these lessons, because they contain within them the seeds of future mistakes, captured *without* disastrous consequences. In fact, this is the perfect time to attack the root causes of these future disasters. As the article's author points out, "latent errors often exist for long periods of time before they combine with enabling conditions to produce a significant failure ... It makes little sense to try to predict or control enabling conditions. Instead, companies should focus on identifying and fixing latent errors before circumstances allow them to create a crisis."[6]

There are some important lessons to draw from this insight. First, near misses can often look like successes, but they're not. Second, it's in our interest to investigate even the small-scale setback as if it were a big one. So the next time you experience a close call, run a quick counter factual analysis to assess what might have been; you'll be glad that you did.

MM HABIT 5: SET A GOAL FOR EVERYONE TO MAKE ONE NEW MISTAKE A WEEK

A core tenet of the Magnificent Mistake™ philosophy is succinctly captured in Esther Dyson's admonition to "always make new mistakes." I have spoken at length about how frustrating, and utterly avoidable, repeated errors are, and clearly I'm on a crusade to eliminate them. What might seem less obvious, though, is the equally sensible advice to consistently be wrong in your life and career.

Let me explain. Another way of wording this direction is to make useful mistakes. It's critical to make missteps because if we don't, it means we're not taking enough risks. You need the members of your team to stretch out of their comfort zone from time to time. While they will doubtlessly come up short now and again, this is also the only way you can spur the innovation and game-changing product or service you need to stay competitive. You should task your team to make one new mistake a week. This translates into 12 miscues a quarter and 50 new ones a year. This will ensure responsible risk-taking is encouraged in your organization; it will also prompt learning from previous errors, as old mistakes won't count towards this counter-intuitive quota.

Now making one mistake a week may not be a realistic metric for a Fortune 500 company — or even for a small family business — but tell that to the executives at Pixar, the world's most successful animated film company. When they produce their films, they create storyboards of each scene that are then improved and redrawn. Every iteration removes a mistake but may create another. Pixar employees are apparently pretty comfortable committing errors this way, as *Finding Nemo* took 43,536 storyboards to complete while *Wall-E* required an astounding 98,173.[7] The next time you're admonishing an employee for making a mistake, remember the advice of former Formula One driver Mario Andretti: "if everything seems under control, you're not going fast enough."

MM HABIT 6: BE ON THE LOOK OUT FOR BRILLIANT ACCIDENTS.
HAVE YOUR TEAM SHOW YOU THEIR CRUMPLED BALLS OF PAPER
"We learned much more from failed new brands and products like Dryel at-home dry cleaning and Fit Fruit & Vegetable Wash than we did from huge successes like Febreze and Swiffer." **A.G. Lafley**, **Former Procter & Gamble CEO**

When you think about it, A.G. Lafley has exactly the right attitude toward defeat. As he puts it, "we learn much more from failure than we do success."

I couldn't agree more (and wrote the book you're holding to expand on the idea and explore how to do just that). But it begs another question: what is your organization failing to learn from right now?

You never know if a vital lesson, or a brilliant product, is hidden inside the crumpled pieces of paper in your employees' waste paper baskets. So it's a good move to ask to see your employees' discarded ideas from time to time.

These might turn out to be 'Intelligent Failures'.[8] Duke University Professor Sim Sitkin coined this phrase to describe mistakes that are good because they provide valuable new knowledge. They could do so by showing how not to do something. These rough drafts may alternatively point the way to a new product or service — a direction for your company that's worthwhile but simply ahead of its time. The Newton Personal Digital Assistant was an abject flop for Apple at the time of its discontinuation in 1998, but it paved the way for the development of the iPad a decade later. 3M famously turned an ineffective adhesive into the glue that fastens the Post-It Notes to your papers today. Sometimes when you attempt fails to resolve one issue, you might discover that you actually found an imaginative answer to a totally different question. So what are the billion dollar ideas hiding in your company trash baskets?

First drafts are not just for writers. In order to tap into these imperfect initial tries, however, one must build a culture that accepts and even celebrates such productive errors. Organizations succeed in promoting ambitious innovation when they reduce the stigma of mistakes. For example, pharmaceutical leader Eli Lilly has long held 'failure parties' to single out intelligent risks: worthwhile and well-conceived experiments that fail to achieve the desired results. Share those mistakes, too. One company has a wall where they write down their errors so that others can learn from them. Change the culture of your organization so that they embrace the wisdom mistakes can provide — if properly leveraged, of course.

Get in the habit of encouraging your team to take smart swings for the fences, and do what one key executive asks his reports to do during performance reviews: "show me your scrap heap."

MM HABIT 7: EVEN IF IT ISN'T BROKEN ... ACT LIKE IT IS: RED TEAM EVERYTHING

Don't stop with simply celebrating failure. It's also important to stress-test success. One does so by adopting a policy of systematic analysis ... even when things are going well. This is where yet another benefit of mistakes can — and should — be harnessed. When a move turns out to be a winner, few do a formal review to capture its lessons. This is will enable you to test theories about what is contributing to today's success (or failure), as well as what can help you achieve better performance in the future.

As Harvard Business School professors Francesca Gino and Gary Pisano note, "managers must actively test their theories, even when they seem to be working, and rigorously investigate the causes of both good and bad performance."[9]

The term 'red team' comes from the military. The U.S. Army defines red teaming as a "structured, iterative process executed by trained, educated and practiced team members that provide commanders an independent capability to continuously challenge plans, operations, concepts, organizations and capabilities in the context of the operational environment and from our partners' and adversaries' perspectives."

While this concept has had its original application in military war games, the idea has increasingly come to be used in business, politics and the media as well. The core principle it evokes is the reflex to challenge every assumption, sacrifice every sacred cow, and to question every certainty. You can put this into practice by establishing red teams to make the devil's advocate case against every major decision you consider taking. You don't have to create contrarian views if they already exist in your organization, too: all you have to do is make sure to solicit them. The general point is that red teaming is a critical and prudent way to assess options.

You might consider going even further by creating units within your organization that brainstorm about how a competitor might attack your market position. It's all about fighting the complacency success brings, and constantly being aware the foundation on which your current state rests is fragile — more sand than cement.

Indeed, your organization should get into the habit of evaluating projects at every stage of their development, up to and including when they've been deemed a success. The chief knowledge officer at NASA's Goddard Space Flight Centre, Edward Rogers, for instance, instituted a 'pause and learn' process in which teams discuss at each project milestone what they have learned. "Almost every mishap at NASA can be traced to some series of small signals that went unnoticed at the critical moment," he says.

You would do well to follow the examples of NASA and the Pentagon. Don't rest on your laurels; develop the organizational reflex to be paranoid and skeptical. Follow the fictional Fox Mulder's mantra from the TV series *The X-Files*: "question everything."

MM Habit 8: Put out a quarterly Failure Report and keep a Mistake Journal™

Engineers without Borders (EWB) is a world-class organization started in Canada in 2000 by University of Waterloo engineering students Parker Mitchell and George Roter. In less than a decade, they grew their operation to harness the power of 45,000 members ands 3,000 volunteers lending their engineering expertise to trouble spots in the developing world. In so doing, they have pioneered their own formula for intelligent development, where they focus on prototyping and then piloting systemic innovations that can be scaled to the mass market. It is in this area where their unique approach to mistakes can set an example; as they describe it: "we test small to determine viability at low cost, providing support as our partner leads. Failure means we learn and return to prototype. Success means we refine and multiply."[10]

EWB is remarkably candid about their mistakes. In fact, every year since 2008 they have published "Failure Reports," detailing everything from prosaic errors made in the construction of roads, to more fundamental breakdowns of communication between the local teams and head office.

EWB isn't the only organization that's failing; but it *is* the only one that is completely transparent about its failures. Take heed of their example, and adopt the practice for your own outfit.

As well, build your 'data base' of chronic mistakes. Keep a Mistake Journal™ (*for a sample page, go to The Magnificent Mistake™ Workbook on my website, www.IonValis.com*). Then build a set of scripts for what to do when you spot these traps in the future. What we need is a tripwire — one that's triggered by recognizing the pattern that preceded your previous mistakes. We want to introduce circuit breakers into your system, and the Mistake Journal™ will give you the framework to capture those lessons for the future.

The more candid you are about your misfires, the more likely you will be able to extract the wisdom from these experiences. Sometimes, that can literally affect the lives of yours customers.

In 2014, it came to light that General Motors (GM) had been hiding a fault in their ignition system that had been identified as far back as 2002. If GM had adopted the openness we preach as part of its culture, perhaps some, if not all, of the over 50 crashes and 21 tragic deaths already tied to this known defect could have been avoided. In discussing the institutional failures that led to this catastrophic collective loss of judgment, GM CEO Mary Barra underscored the dangers of hiding mistakes: "Numerous individuals did not accept any responsibility to drive our organization to understand what was truly happening. The report highlights a company that operated in silos, with a number of individuals seemingly looking for reasons not to act, instead of finding ways to protect our customers."

Learn from GM's mistake: instituting a regular 'mistake mea culpa' will demonstrate humility and transparency while promoting risk-taking and learning. So don't bury your errors; catalogue and communicate them across the organization.

You'll be shocked at how much goodwill, and good ideas, will arise as a result, and you might save lives and your company's good name in the process.

MM HABIT 9: HAVE YOUR TEAM HAVE A TO NOT DO LIST ALONGSIDE THEIR TO DO LIST

As Tom Peters points out in *The Little BIG Things: 163 Ways to Pursue Excellence,* what you decide *not* to do often has more impact than what you decide to do. As he puts it, 'To Don'ts' are more important than 'To Dos'.

In today's world of infinite choice and distractions, 'no' is your most powerful productivity move. Forget your organization apps and lists; the most useful tool to get the right things done is your wastepaper basket. The more you say no to opportunities and offers, the more time, focus and energy you have to devote to the tasks that matter. That's why one of Steve Jobs' 7 key principles to great innovation was to "say no to a 1,000 things and think differently about design."

No one is as productive as they can be. We all get distracted by the beep of a new text message or the rabbit hole of an Internet article's endless hyperlinks. By keeping track of the things that detract from doing important work you increase the likelihood of staying on task. Adopting this one habit will increase your team's personal productivity more than any fancy task management software.

There's another reason to start this list, however. More than simply staying away from time or focus wasters, this practice can also tap the wisdom of earlier iterations. Business schools teach the virtues of 'second-mover advantage,' where it's not always better to come first. This is the case when the second company to introduce an innovative product or service can learn from the mistakes of the pioneering one. We've seen this throughout business history, where the iPod improved on the first MP3 players, or when Facebook built on its predecessor Friendster by offering a more compelling social network. It never pays just to imitate, but it does pay off to improve on the products or services that came before.

Ultimately, one can learn as much from the 'How-not-to' as much as the 'How-to' and compiling a 'To Don't' List is a great place to start.

MM Habit 10: Make MMs part of your team's KPIs

I've introduced the concept of a magnificent mistake in this book, and it can most succinctly be described in the following equation:

$$\text{Error} + \text{Learning} = \text{Magnificent Mistake}$$

The idea is simple to grasp, and easy to execute with the M.A.S.T.E.R.™ Checklist. So why don't you mandate your team consistently turn their missteps into Magnificent Mistakes (MMs) as part of their quarterly or annual Key Performance Indicators (KPIs)?

Answering this call to action forces them to implement the checklist and systematically learn from their errors — or those of your competitors. Remember sometimes we don't even have to be the ones to actually make the mistake to learn from them; using the checklist to analyze the missteps of your rivals can be an incredible source of competitive advantage over the long run.

So ask your reports: How many MMs did you have this quarter? In doing so, you'll be creating the foundation for the larger habit to take root, so at some point every one of their errors will be analyzed in this way. Capturing the wisdom of errors can only benefit your organization, and the best way to start that practice is to insist on it until it becomes second nature.

MM HABIT 11: DON'T TREAT ALL ERRORS EQUALLY
This next habit runs a little counter to all of the ones that have come before, but it does so for a purpose. I have consistently argued throughout this book we need to change — even reverse — the way we look at mistakes: we should see them as blessings, not burdens, while letting our employees have the freedom to fail.

This remains true, up to a point. Some mistakes can't be made magnificent — at least not for the organization that makes them. Committing certain errors even one time is once too many. Not all miscues are created equal. If you're the CEO of an airline company, your employees need to realize the difference between losing a bag and crashing a plane. This may seem obvious to you, but there is a real danger if you signal *some* mistakes are ok, you may in fact weaken their vigilance against other, more critical ones.

Even though one wants to create an organizational culture that is tolerant of failure, it is still incumbent on the leader to communicate precisely when certain mistakes are acceptable (and when then are not).

The need to create an environment providing the psychological safety to make small missteps must therefore also be balanced with clear communication and unwavering accountability. By specifying, and regularly repeating, what *is* and *isn't* acceptable in your organization, you will remove any ambiguity that might arise in an otherwise mistake-friendly workplace. By sanctioning more serious errors with appropriate punishments, a leader will signal what cannot be tolerated — under *any* circumstance.

This is a necessary counter-measure to the previous Magnificent Mistake Habits™ and it is critical to properly calibrate your organization's attitude towards error.

MM HABIT 12: HIRE WITH FAILURE IN MIND — LOOK FOR PEOPLE WHO HAVE FAILED TWICE OVER THOSE WHO HAVE SUCCEEDED ONCE

After establishing a Magnificent Mistake™ culture in your organization, you will want to preserve and protect it by hiring 'the right kind of people.' Ideally, you will look for candidates who have a healthy relationship with failure. This means not only that they have experienced it (after all, everyone has), but especially that they have faced and learned from it.

In your next interview, instead of asking "what is your biggest weakness?" (and getting the answer "I'm a perfectionist!" back), prompt the applicant to talk about a major mistake he or she made, and specifically how and what they learned from it. This line of questioning will reveal a number of important characteristics of your candidate, namely whether or not they are humble, introspective and adaptable.

One CEO, Richard Guha, goes even further: he states flatly that he'd "rather hire someone who has failed twice than succeeded once."[11]

THE LAST WORD

This chapter provides a dozen habits of thought and mind that will help you in the classroom, the boardroom or simply the living room. Over time, I hope that this new mindset becomes second nature and part of your weekly, monthly and annual routine (*for more information on how to implement these habits, go to Part III of the book*). The 12 Magnificent Mistake Habits™ should be added to your toolkit, whether you're a parent, part-time coach or president of a company. They are great practices to sharpen your edge as a leader, stay on top of performance issues for yourself and your team, and promote accountability, innovation and overall organizational effectiveness.

One final note: the example set by senior leaders like you will be crucial before any of these behaviors can set in. You must show that it's okay to admit to mistakes by doing it yourself. So start by living the 12 Habits yourself before asking others to adopt them; you will benefit from their practice, and the organization you lead will come to blossom from them as well. Remember: the transformation the Magnificent Mistake™ approach brings shouldn't end with you. If you lead in any way — a family, a flag football team, a foundation or a Fortune 500 company — the next step is to apply these tools and principles to your leadership philosophy.

CHAPTER FOUR - THE SPEED READ

IN A NUTSHELL:

One can generate a wealth of wisdom from a new perspective on error. In addition, applying this principle in your professional activities can yield even larger-scale improvements. Applying the 12 Magnificent Mistake Habits™ to your organization will make your team or company more accountable, more innovative, and more effective.

POINTS TO PONDER:

✔ Give your team permission to screw up. Studies show when people feel they are allowed to make mistakes, they are significantly less likely to actually make them.

✔ You never know if a vital lesson — or a brilliant product — is hidden inside the crumpled pieces of paper in your employees' waste paper baskets. So it's a good move to ask to see your employees' discarded ideas from time to time.

✔ Don't stop with simply celebrating failure. It's also important to stress-test success. Challenge every assumption, sacrifice every sacred cow and question every 'certainty'.

PUTTING IT INTO PRACTICE:

➤ Implement the 12 Magnificent Mistake Organizational Habits™ in your team or company environment.

➤ Teach it to others. One of the quickest ways to learn something new, and to practice it, is to show others how to do it. Share what you learn with your team, your manager, or your co-workers.

CONCLUSION

THE END OF MERE ERRORS, THE BEGINNING OF MAGNIFICENT MISTAKES

London, July 2012. A talented American swimmer comes to the Olympics after months of magazine covers touting him as the king of swim. According to these breathless scouting reports, he's certain to build on his success in Beijing and be the star of these Games. Records will be broken and multiple gold medals will be won, they say; the only question is how many can he collect?

If this sounds to you like the run-up to the 2008 Beijing Olympics, you're in good company. Michael Phelps felt the same way — only this time these stories were about his teammate yet arch-rival Ryan Lochte, the new darling of American swimming. It was Lotto, not Phelps, who rode into London that summer on a wave of hype and hope. Many experts were wondering aloud whether Phelps, at 28 but competing in his fourth Olympiad, had made a mistake in coming back to the pool. The results in their first head to head final didn't contradict that initial verdict, either. In what was seen as a generational passing of the torch, Lochte blew past all competition and won gold in the 400 IM (international medley), relegating a despondent Phelps to fourth and out of the medal round.

The media reaction was instantaneous. Lochte was the 'new' Phelps, and Phelps was, well, old. The BBC announced Lotto had "thrashed his compatriot," and Phelps' lackadaisical display "raised questions about his form." Indeed, Phelps and his longtime coach, Bob Bowman, seemed to be in shock. Bowman said after the race that his star pupil had "trained really well coming in here. I'm surprised. We just have to put it behind us and move on."

Many people probably wrote Michael Phelps off that evening, presuming even great champions sometimes overstay their time on the podium. Phelps himself might have been tempted, for a moment, to surrender to the inevitability of age and leave the stage to his rival.

But champions don't become great by staying down after being knocked down, as we've learned. True legends of their sport use those setbacks to fuel their next success, as did Michael Phelps. After that race, he said: "The biggest thing now is to try to get past this and move forward. I have a bunch of other races and hopefully we can finish a lot better than when we started."

In their next race, this time as teammates, in the 4 x 100 freestyle relay, it was Phelps, not Lochte, who swam masterfully. He clocked the fastest leg on the team and set the table for Lochte to bring home the gold in his anchor leg. From that point on, Phelps won 4 gold medals and two silver en route to finishing the Olympics as the most successful swimmer (6 medals) in London but also the greatest Olympian of all time (22 medals, 18 of them gold). Lochte finished with 2 gold, 2 silver and a bronze medal. While Phelps' London haul didn't match his record eight gold medals from Beijing four years prior, he still ruled the pool. As the *San Jose Mercury News* put it in summing up his Games, "Phelps' redemption came after finishing fourth on opening day in the 400 individual medley. Since then he [was] superb every time he leapt off the starting block."

Michael Phelps knows how to handle mistakes. Faced with a humiliating defeat at the beginning of his final Olympics, he could have blown off the rest of his races. He could have given in to the temptation to 'accept' being older and slower in the pool. Instead, he did what he's often done when faced with setbacks — what outstanding performers in sports, business and in life always do: he internalized the lessons of his failure and quickly forgot about the mistake.

I begin and end this book with anecdotes about the greatest Olympian of all time because I believe that we can learn a thing or two about peak performance from Michael Phelps. We may not compete in global athletic competitions like he did, or invest millions of dollars like Warren Buffett; but we do face our own contests, however small or large, every single day. We all feel the sting of defeat, though it may be on a less public scale. We also have to decide how we will react to obstacles when they occur in our personal or professional lives. Normal people encounter failure in every possible way, even if gold medals or golden paydays are not always in play. When we do, we should respond like Phelps and Buffett do — not because they are Michael Phelps and Warren Buffett, but because it works.

Every person tells a different story when they talk about their biggest mistakes. But in a larger sense, every error tale is the same: we failed at something and it cost us dearly. We regret having committed it, and we wish that we had the opportunity to go back in time and not make it in the first place.

Sadly, life doesn't give us any real second chances. We can't undo what's been done. We can only move forward, armed with the hard-earned wisdom our miscues have given us. But we have to *choose* to do so; this won't happen on its own. Only by admitting, accepting, and analyzing our miscues can we hope to move past them.

Errors are inevitable. They can be reduced, but they can never be eliminated. We all make mistakes. But how you handle those mistakes makes all the difference. What I've tried to put forward in this book is that while we can never erase a mistake, we can make them become magnificent in hindsight. In so doing, we change the way we regard that failure and begin to see it for what it is: the first step to success. 'Mistake' is a negative word, but it doesn't have to be. People instantly flinch at the sound of the term, but I want to transform your reaction into a more positive one — closer to 'opportunity' or 'wisdom'. On a philosophical level, my approach is all about injecting meaning into your mistake. Errors will always happen; but what good is a failure if you don't learn from it? The Magnificent Mistake™ practice allows you to make them purposeful.

Learning from your mistakes is timeless good advice. In fact, we're living proof this is so: we're standing here today because our ancestors learned from the mistakes of others — the caveman who ran faster from the saber-tooth tiger than his cousin, for example. This will always be true, and it will always be the easiest first step towards improving performance. This bit of common sense can be used by beginners but is also employed quite effectively by the pros: in fact, that's how they become pros and stay ahead of the competition. It's so intuitive yet so effective. It's not the 'new new thing' ... But it works. Period.

At the end of the day, the question of whether or not to adopt this approach rests on two simple arguments: what's the cost? And what's the alternative? It costs you nothing, and the alternative is to do nothing — and keep making those same errors even though you don't have to.

In the previous pages, I have made a few simple arguments. First, expect errors and embrace them. Second, learn from your mistakes (and I go into detail about why and how). Third, make fewer of those mistakes. Repeat. Finally, we have more to earn from failure than we can learn from success.

Mistakes present a great opportunity to learn and improve, but action is required. This starts by making a simple choice to tap the power of your mistakes in a way you haven't before. It means deciding you want to finally leverage the lessons of losses and defeats. Instead of starting with success and working backwards, start with failure and move forward. Resist the siren song of success stories. Focus instead on a strategy built on the small wins of mastering your mistakes one by one.

Studying failure or success is a false choice. You should do both, but we rarely do either. A better approach is to put both on an equal footing. Both should trigger further investigation that helps us revise our assumptions, models and theories. Celebrate success, but examine it. When you get a big win, study what led to it with the same rigor and scrutiny that you would apply to understanding why you might have failed. By the same token, examine failure, but also celebrate it — for all the reasons we've discussed.

I've distilled the best practices of the top individuals, organizations and institutions into a strategic framework you can easily apply to any mistake, small or large. The M.A.S.T.E.R.™ Checklist is a simple yet potentially very powerful methodology. It will provide results that will pay off instantly if you use it to leverage mistakes and capture wisdom. But it has to be used frequently, formally and systematically. If you do, I know that the tools in this book can improve your personal life as well as your professional career. This isn't just good for business; it's good for our life as well.

MAKE BETTER MISTAKES TOMORROW

In many ways, we are defined by our mistakes ...but we don't have to be. Actress Tallulah Bankhead wasn't; that comes out clearly in her rueful observation: "if I had to live my life again, I'd make the same mistakes, only sooner."

She recognized mistakes are the ultimate teaching moments. This is not a new view; indeed, such observations have been accepted wisdom for centuries, if not millennia. Why else would a Greek sage like Euripides remark: "if we could be twice young and twice old, we could correct all our mistakes."

On some level, this idea might seem obvious to you. Learning from mistakes is a great success strategy, yet most people consistently fail to follow this advice. But that's not a good reason to ignore what we've discovered, namely this is the secret to most individuals and organizations' continued improvement. This best practice comes into sharp relief when you study the top performers in almost every field, and not just because it is what got them there. It's also what's keeping them there. For a lot of organizations, success begins from learning from their mistakes, and those of their competitors. For others, it's how they sustain success.

The benefits of making fewer errors — and preventing repeated ones — seem obvious. Yet people don't know why it's so important, and who among their sports heroes and business competitors are actually doing this regularly, or even how to do it quickly, efficiently but effectively. With this book, now they do. Once a small amount of initial effort is invested to understand the process and make it a habit, you can reap its benefits time after time ... and mistake after mistake.

LEARN ... OR LOSE

Thermodynamics is the branch of physics concerned with energy. Its first law states energy can be transformed but it cannot be created or destroyed. It appears the same is true with mistakes.

Put another way, mistakes have what I call an obsidian quality to them. I discovered this on my way to visit Chichen Itza, Mexico in February 2010. According to Mayan custom, obsidian stone turns negative energy into positive. It has the physical property of being black but looks silver in the sunlight. It's an apt metaphor for what I think the Magnificent Mistake™ approach can do for mistakes.

The central idea of this book is this: the difference between an error and a Magnificent Mistake™ is whether you learn from it.

However, it doesn't just occur automatically: you have to transform the error into a Magnificent Mistake™. It is a deliberate, conscious and systematic process, and we must have the will and skill to make it happen.

I've attempted to provide you with a tool to do just that. In my thinking on the subject, I've come to believe that a framework for learning from mistakes must be:
- A conscious choice
- Systematic and habitual
- Intellectually rigorous
- Comprehensive

- Simple and straightforward enough to perform quickly
- Sophisticated enough to be applied to complex failures and large organizations

The best method is the one that is effective, easy to execute and repeat, and also one you will remember to use and return to often.

The Magnificent Mistake™ philosophy is all of these things. It is contrarian, as opposed to conventional, wisdom; but it's also meant to be practical. For extra measure, it also is a well-designed progression: each step builds upon the previous one and follows a prescribed sequence. In fact, the progression won't allow you to move on to the next stage until you completed the last one. The steps in the checklist are layered.

Finally, it is both a concept and a system. The concept is simple: you transform errors into magnificent mistakes by learning valuable lessons from them and then avoid repeating them in the future. The system is made up of the 6-step M.A.S.T.E.R.™ Checklist, the 12 Habits for Teams and Organizations as well as the 12 Magnificent Mistake Principles™ (*all found in Part III, "Applying The Magnificent Mistake to Living and Leading"*). These tools can be added to your bag of tricks as a parent, teacher or leader ... but the philosophy could also change your career and your life.

I'm not an expert on success, but I do know something about failure. Learning from your own mistakes is good. Learning from others' mistakes is better. Learning from both is best. Or, as a famous proverb puts it: "wise men learn by other men's mistakes, fools by their own."

As Google executives like to say, life is a permanent beta. You need to be constantly improving, revising and re-engineering, just like those apps you download onto your iPhone that are regularly updated. And you do that by tackling your errors. That's what the Magnificent Mistake™ practice seeks to achieve: version 2.0 of you and your mistakes, made-over.

A FINAL (PERSONAL) WORD

I've had three mini-careers so far, and I've embarked on my fourth now with this book. I'm hoping the majority of my failures are behind me ... but I know how to learn from them if they aren't, and why it's so important to do so. Someone once noted it took ten years to become an overnight success; it might also be said it takes hundreds of mistakes as well.

Mistakes have made me the man that I am, for better and, sometimes, for worse. But errors don't need to be epitaphs. You can't change the past, but you can redefine its legacy. After all, "creativity is allowing yourself to make mistakes. Art is knowing which ones to keep."

This book is probably full of mistakes ... but I'll learn from them. Will you?

PART III:
APPLYING *THE MAGNIFICENT MISTAKE* TO LIVING AND LEADING

THE M.A.S.T.E.R.™ CHECKLIST

M.A.S.T.E.R.™ is simple enough to remember easily and do on the spot; nimble enough to apply to big mistakes as well as small blunders; and comprehensive enough to make sure you are capturing the right lessons and incorporating them into future decisions.

M - **Make** peace with your mistake.
A - **Analyze** it.
S - **Search** for the key cause by identifying the *Error Gene*™.
T - **Take in** the right lesson(s).
E - **Eliminate** the *Error Gene*™, then **Erase** the mistake.
R - **Reprogram** yourself to spot and sidestep that error in the future. **Repeat.**

THE 12 MAGNIFICENT MISTAKE™ PRINCIPLES

I – We can earn more from failure than we learn from success.
II – Success is not what it seems. It surprises, is often serendipitous and spontaneous, is the sum of small steps (as opposed to the result of a single, seismic event) and is frequently a singular and short-lived event.
III – Focus on failure instead of studying success.
IV – Always make new mistakes.
V – One of the best-kept secrets of truly successful people and organizations is they systematically learn from their mistakes.
VI – Learning from mistakes is a skill — one of the key factors in determining long-term success in every walk of life, from sports to business. It's also a skill that can be learned, honed and perfected.
VII – There is a difference between knowing what to do ... and doing what you know. A formalized process is the key to properly learning from mistakes. It's not just having a well thought-out procedure in place that matters, but also that it is applied automatically and without exception after every error.
VIII – The best approaches to reviewing errors are systematic, refined over time, structured, objective, focus on capturing knowledge and on applying the lessons to a larger context. They also seek to be comprehensive, consider all opinions and produce a series of actionable prescriptions designed to prevent repeating the error.
IX – M.A.S.T.E.R.™ your mistakes.
X – Practice and pass on the 12 Magnificent Mistake Habits™.

XI – Examine failure, but also celebrate it; celebrate success, but also examine it.

XII – Learning from your own mistakes is good; learning from others' mistakes is better; learning from both is best

THE 12 MAGNIFICENT MISTAKE HABITS™

1 – Don't fear failure or wait for a perfect moment: apply the 70% Rule.

2 – Focus on getting better rather than being good.

3 – Study your successes this way, too.

4 – Make the most of your near misses.

5 – Set a goal to make one new mistake a week.

6 – Be on the lookout for Brilliant Accidents: have your team show you their crumpled balls of paper.

7 – Even if it isn't broken, act like it is: Red Team everything.

8 – Put out a quarterly Failure Report and keep a Mistake Journal™.

9 – Have a To Not Do List.

10 – Make MMs part of your team's KPIs.

11 – Don't treat all errors equally.

12 – Hire with failure in mind: look for people who have failed twice over those who have succeeded once.

HOW TO COMMUNICATE
THE IDEAS FROM
THE MAGNIFICENT MISTAKE

THE TWITTER SUMMARY (140 CHARACTERS + LINK TO URL AND HASHTAG)

@IonValis: The diff between an error and a Magnificent Mistake is whether you learn from it. Here's how: www.MagnificentMistake.com #MakeMagnificentMistakes

@IonValis: We have more to EARN from Failure than we can LEARN from Success. See how: www.MagnificentMistake.com #MagnificentMistake

@IonValis: Here's how to master and make the most of your mistakes: www.MagnificentMistake.com #MakeMagnificentMistakes

@IonValis: Don't just manage your mistakes: M.A.S.T.E.R. them. This will change how you run your career, family, team or company. Here's how: www.MagnificentMistake.com #MakeMagnificentMistakes

@IonValis: Learning from mistakes is the fastest, simplest, most powerful and yet least practiced way to improve you or your organization's performance. Here's how: www.MagnificentMistake.com #MagnificentMistake

@IonValis: The big idea is this: One of the best-kept secrets of truly successful people and organizations is that they systematically learn from their mistakes. Here's how: www.MagnificentMistake.com #MagnificentMistake

@IonValis: Focusing on failures — yours and your competitors — is your first step to success. Here's how: www.MagnificentMistake.com #MagnificentMistake

@IonValis: Discover how to M.A.S.T.E.R. your mistakes and develop the 12 Magnificent Mistake Habits for Teams and Organizations. Here's how: www.MagnificentMistake.com #MakeMagnificentMistakes

ELEVATOR RIDE | PITCH SUMMARY (60 WORDS, OR 20 SECONDS OF TALKING)

Learning from mistakes is a superb strategy for success in your personal and professional life. It is the most direct, most powerful yet least practiced way to improve you or your company's performance. Finally, one of the best-kept secrets of truly successful people and organizations is they habitually and systematically profit from their errors and those of their competitors.

COCKTAIL PARTY SUMMARY (250 WORDS, OR LESS THAN A MINUTE OF TALKING)

They say the only certainties in life are death and taxes. I would add a third: mistakes. We all commit errors — often small ones, sometimes big ones, and all too frequently the same ones.

What if you learned it was actually crucially important to learn from our mistakes, and that we can, in fact, earn more from failure than we learn from success? What if you knew that top performing individuals and institutions — the most successful people and organizations in the world — did just that, and it is often the secret sauce to their success? Finally, what if someone gave you a simple way to quickly draw the right lesson from your errors — a six-step checklist captured in the acronym M.A.S.T.E.R.™ — that you could turn to after an annoying little miscue at home or a massive failure at work?

We know intuitively we should learn from our missteps. However, very few of us actually do, and that itself is a huge error. All great achievers, teams and companies share one common trait — they have the discipline to systematically learn from mistakes (theirs, and their competitors). It's also the fastest, simplest, most powerful and yet least practiced way to improve you or your organization's performance.

Whether you're an entrepreneur, an employee or an executive, this book is for you. The ripple effect of learning how to M.A.S.T.E.R.™ your mistakes will help you become a better teammate, improve your performance at work ... and could change your life.

THE MAGNIFICENT MISTAKE™ IN EQUATIONS:

Some people understand concepts better visually, so I've provided some of the key ideas from the book in the form of equations. I am indebted to Chip Conley's excellent *Emotional Equations* for the counter-intuitive idea of expressing complex thoughts in such a graphic fashion.

Error + Learning = **Magnificent Mistake™ (MM)**
Error - Learning = **Repeating Mistakes**
MM + MM + MM ... = **Continuous Improvement**

THE GLOSSARY OF TERMS AND CONCEPTS

2 Whats

These are the two questions that you must ask yourself before undertaking any analysis of a mistake. Its use serves to remind you what the objective of the activity that originally went wrong was; this will ensure you are focused on asking the right questions going forward. So ask yourself at the outset:

1) *What did you set out to do?*
2) *What actually happened?*

4 Cs and the 3Is

These are two tools to easily remember the key steps in taking in the lessons of your mistake. It seems obvious, but the whole point of learning something is to improve performance in the future. The hard-earned knowledge you've just extracted from your mistake will only be useful if you do something with it. So you have to *capture, crystallize, commit* and *communicate* what you've learned. *Capturing* the lesson is memorializing the specific cause and effect relationship ("I crashed when I took my eyes off the road to return a txt message.") Then you have to distill the take-away into the most succinct prescriptive formulation possible by *crystallizing* it down to its essence ("Don't txt and drive — period."). You subsequently *commit* to the direction in a clear expression of resolve ("I will never txt while driving.") Finally, *communicate* this new rule where and when necessary ("I swear to you, Mom, I will never txt again while driving.")

There are a few other steps if you are addressing an error that has affected others, or that should be shared across an organization. In this case, you must *incorporate* and *institutionalize* the lessons learned *immediately*. (3Is)

5 Whys
A technique developed by Toyota Motor Company and frequently used in engineering circles to get to the root cause of a problem. It consists of asking the question "why?" five times in a row in an attempt to get to the root cause of a problem.

70% Rule
The Marine Corps believe in getting just the right amount of information they need before mobilizing. This bias for action is especially prevalent in the planning stage of an operation, and the formula they follow is simple: if you have 70% of the data, have done 70% of the analysis, and feel 70% confident, then make your move.

For the Marines, the decision point comes after crossing a threshold of optimal information; they choose to optimize rather than maximize their preparations before engaging. They realize a less than ideal action, swiftly executed, stands some chance of success — while the worst move is to make no decision at all.

After-Action Review (AAR)
The AAR has become a staple of Army procedure since it was introduced as a practice and learning tool after the Vietnam War. As defined by the Army, an AAR is a professional discussion of an event, focused on performance standards, allowing participants to discover from themselves what happened, why

it happened, and how to sustain strengths and improve on weaknesses ... Formal AARs are scheduled after each mission and can last a few hours; informal AARs are run consistently after other events, even if they are five minute reviews to build on lessons learned.

Collection of Errors (CoE)
Amazon employees rely on this little publicized but often used process to analyze and address mistakes made (it is described extensively in Chapter 2).

Compound Consequences (CCs)
These are the second and third order effects of your decision(s). The CCs can be found in the downstream impact of a choice, or series of choices, that combine and grow quickly (like compound interest) to create a particularly negative situation. In cataloguing the CCs of a specific wrong decision, you can capture the extent of an error's impact. By doing so, you will reduce the possibility related mistakes are treated separately.

Critical Failure Factors (CFFs)
These are the key decisions, moments or events where things began to go wrong. They represent the opposite of their significantly better-known cousin, the Critical Success Factor. Another way of characterizing them is as the 'strategic inflection points' (a term popularized by Andy Grove, the CEO of Intel) that lead to a mistake, defeat or failure.

Error Gene^{TM}
The Error Gene^{TM} is the label I've developed to describe the true source of a mistake. When performing your analysis

in Step 3 (Search for the key cause) of the M.A.S.T.E.R.™ Checklist, the Error Gene™ is what one is left with once you've stripped away all of the other possible factors at play. It's the most irreducible part of your mistake, and the key variable that drove you to misstep. It is also, therefore, the specific bias, behavior or miscalculation you have to eliminate going forward if you are to avoid that type of mistake in the future.

Failure
Failure is the state or condition of not meeting a desired or intended objective, and may be viewed as the opposite of success. It can also describe a chain of smaller mistakes that, when combined, produced a systemic failure.

<u>Note</u>: The difference between Mistake and Failure
These two words should not be used interchangeably. There are multiple levels of difference between a mistake and a failure. There is a quantitative element: a mistake is single act or event, whereas a failure can contain within it a number of mistakes. There is also a qualitative element: a mistake may be small, whereas a failure is always significant. Finally, there is a time dimension difference as well. A mistake occurs in a precise moment, like a quarterback throwing an interception; a failure occurs over time.

Mistakes sometimes cause a failure, but a failure never causes a mistake. A mistake gone continuously uncorrected ultimately results in failure. However, failures don't always stem from mistakes and sometimes they simply cannot be avoided.

Both success and failure are outcomes. A failure — to end without success — can occur because of external circumstances; you did everything right and still failed. But a mistake is something for which you are responsible. Failure is subject to external variables whereas as mistakes are internal; you commit them yourself.

Hansei
This is a Japanese term that translates into "relentless reflection."

Jidoka
This is a Japanese term meaning the ability to stop production lines to ensure quality.

Kaizen
This is a Japanese term that translates into "continuous improvement".

Lessons Learned (LLs)
These represent the key takeaways from a given mistake analysis, and they surface as a result of Step 3 (Search for the key cause) and are absorbed in Step 4 (Take in the Right Lessons) of the M.A.S.T.E.R.™ Process. LLs are the output of your examination, but they are also their most important legacy. These lessons — one of which should be the identification of the specific Error Gene™ and Mistake Trap™ associated with this miscue — are the nuggets of wisdom that you've extracted from your misfortune. Discovering and applying these lessons going forward will ensure that you've successfully transformed your error into a Magnificent Mistake™.

Magnificent Mistake™ (MM)
The difference between an error and a Magnificent Mistake™ is whether you learn from it. You transform miscues by drawing

the right lessons from them, thereby making it less likely that you will repeat it in the future.

MM KPIs
Magnificent Mistake Key Performance Indicators (MM KPIs) should be used as part of Habit 10. They consist of creating metrics to measure your own progress — or that of your team or organization — in applying the M.A.S.T.E.R.™ Framework to your mistakes as well as adopting the 12 Magnificent Mistake Habits™.

Mission Failures (MFs)
A Mission Failure is the name for the type of mistake you, your team or organization cannot tolerate. Even though one wants to create an organizational culture tolerant of failure, it is still incumbent on the leader to communicate precisely when certain mistakes are acceptable (and when then are not). Committing certain errors even one time is once too many. If you're the CEO of an airline company, losing a bag is acceptable whereas crashing a plane represents a total Mission Failure.

The need to create an environment providing the psychological safety to make small missteps must therefore also be balanced with clear communication and unwavering accountability. By specifying and regularly repeating what *is* and *isn't* acceptable in your organization, you will remove any ambiguity that might arise in an otherwise mistake-friendly workplace. By sanctioning more serious errors – Mission Failures – with appropriate punishments, a leader will signal what cannot be tolerated under any circumstance.

Mistake

Merriam Webster defines 'mistake' as to:
- Blunder in the choice of
- Misunderstand or misinterpret the meaning or intention of,
- Make a wrong judgment of the character or ability of
- Identify wrongly: confuse with another

The Oxford English Dictionary offers a similar interpretation:
- An act or judgement that is misguided or wrong:
- Something, especially a word, figure, or fact, which is not correct; an inaccuracy.

Thus, a mistake is an incorrect, unwise, or unfortunate act or decision. It can be caused by bad judgment, a lack of information, or a lack of attention to detail. While a mistake can lead to failure, it doesn't always have to end in failure.

I outlined the differences between 'mistake' and 'failure' a little earlier in the definition of the latter term.

<u>Note</u>: On the similarity between 'error' and 'mistake'

'Error' and 'mistake' are two different words that are actually synonyms of each other. They mean the same thing, but are used in different context. It is highly acceptable to use 'error' in formal or technical contexts. In scientific or highly technical terms, the word 'error' is more suitable. In the world of computing and programming, 'error' is the more fitting term to indicate a mistake, or fault, particularly in coding and processes. 'Mistake' is used more in casual English conversation. Interestingly, the origins of both words are similar as well: etymology suggests 'error' was from a Latin word which means 'to wander or stray' while 'mistake' is from a Norse word which means 'wrongly taken'.

Micro Mistake

Micro mistakes are the unremarkable, small errors that cause annoyance more than calamity. Spilling coffee on your shirt is a micro-mistake.

Mistake Journal™

This is a catalogue or diary of mistakes that you've made in the past, and analyzed so you don't repeat them in the future. It highlights what went wrong, the critical failure factors involved, the specific error gene, as well as the mistake trap to be avoided going forward. (*You can see an example of a Mistake Journal™ page in the Magnificent Mistake™ Workbook section of my website www.IonValis.com.*)

Mistake Maps

These are visual tools, charts and diagrams that help guide one's thinking when analyzing a mistake. They will help you ask the right questions, at the right time, in the right sequence. (*You can see examples of Mistake Maps in the Magnificent Mistake™ Workbook section of my website www.IonValis.com.*)

Mistake Trap™

This is a situation or circumstance you should seek to avoid because it has caused you to make a mistake in the past. Because you thoroughly analyzed that error, however, you now recognize the telltale signs of that pitfall and can sidestep it now and in the future.

Near Misses

This describes an instance where you narrowly avoided making a big mistake — or worse. It ends in a successful outcome in which luck played a key role in averting disaster. We usually ignore, at our peril, the little mistakes we make along the way when they don't produce terrible outcomes. However, Near Misses are powerful opportunities for learning because they contain within them the seeds of future mistakes captured without disastrous consequences. In other words, they represent gain without pain.

Red Team | Red Teaming
The term 'red team' comes from the military. The U.S. Army defines red teaming as a "structured, iterative process executed by trained, educated and practiced team members that provide commanders an independent capability to continuously challenge plans, operations, concepts, organizations and capabilities in the context of the operational environment and from our partners' and adversaries' perspectives."

While this concept has had its original application in military war games, the idea has increasingly come to be used in business, politics and the media as well. The core principle it evokes is the reflex to challenge every assumption and question every 'certainty'. You can put this into practice by establishing red teams to make the devil's advocate case against every major decision you consider taking. The general point is that red teaming is a critical and prudent way to assess options.

To Not Do List
Tom Peters coined this concept in his book *The Little BIG Things: 163 Ways to Pursue Excellence.* As he pointed out, what you decide *not* to do often has more impact than what you decide to do. As he puts it, " 'To Don'ts' are more important than To Dos." In today's world of infinite choice and distractions,

saying no is your most powerful productivity move. The more you say no to opportunities and offers, the more time, focus and energy you have to devote to the tasks that *matter*.

Creating a 'To Not Do' List is at the heart of Magnificent Mistake Habit 9. A 'To Not Do' List would consist of the negative behaviors (watch more than 10 hours of TV a week or skipping breakfast every morning) and practices (burying your mistakes rather than studying them) you should stop in order to be more productive.

Quarterly Failure Report

Every year since 2008, the non-profit organization Engineers without Borders have published 'Failure Reports' detailing everything from prosaic errors made in the construction of roads, to more fundamental breakdowns of communication between the local teams and head office. In Magnificent Mistake Habit 8, I propose teams and organizations follow their example and put out quarterly failure reports along their other regular statements to their employees or investors. Not only would this transparency be refreshing, it also would demonstrate humility while promoting both risk-taking and the learning that comes with it. Don't bury your errors; instead, catalogue and communicate them across your organization regularly.

DAILY INSPIRATION
THE MOST MEANINGFUL APHORISMS
ABOUT MISTAKES AND FAILURE

Many people don't recognize the word, but an aphorism is one of those curious concepts in the English language that everyone knows what it is yet no one knows what it's called.

Let me try to do for aphorisms what they do for us, namely make a complicated idea both beautiful and simple. An aphorism is a profound but pithy phrase of wisdom, often perfectly put in a memorable sentence or two. They embody the Jesuits' maxim, so perfectly summed up in the epigram: 'Precision of Thought, Economy of Expression.'

They can be both poetic and prosaic. Some people know them as adages, others as sayings and maxims. The more derisive among us might dismiss them as clichés and fortune cookie messages, while Zen monks recite them as koans and mantras. However you feel about aphorisms, the one undeniable reality is that they've been around as long as man has been able to think and speak (in that order).

Socrates gave us one of Western history's first recorded aphorisms when he noted — almost as a coda for future aphorists — "the unexamined life is not worth living." That's essentially what aphorists do: they examine a particular aspect of life and distill it into a pointed or poignant phrase that captures, and delivers, an enormous amount of wisdom in a wonderfully economical way.

Aphorisms are examples of style and substance, form and function; they deliver more punch in a phrase than most writers do in a page. Aphorisms are also, quite accidentally, perhaps the perfect antidote to our current attention-deficit-addled age. This is because they have the unique capability of passing on profound lessons in incredibly concise doses. In an era characterized (and cursed) by six-second attention spans, aphorisms deliver valuable advice in short bursts. Twitter, IM and SMS are the most important media to this generation, and even these limited text technologies can be used to deliver these concise nuggets of wisdom.

Aphorisms provide you with a roadmap to life, giving you turn-by-turn directions to navigate around almost any obstacle. Aphorisms don't just help you with the challenges that life throws at you; they can also teach you how to enjoy life itself. They don't always come inscribed on stone tablets or in musty old tomes, either. One of the simplest, but paradoxically most profound, pieces of wisdom I've ever received came from a lyric in a Sheryl Crow song, namely "happiness is wanting what you have, not getting what you want."

I wish that I had discovered aphorisms earlier in life. After all, aphorisms are essentially attempts by their authors to pass on for free the hard-earned wisdom for which they paid dearly. Why not take them up on their generous offer? These phrases deliver trenchant, and sometimes transcendental, truths that are perfectly suited for this era of Twitter-length attention spans.

For that reason alone, I have collected together the most meaningful quotations addressing the issue of mistakes and failure. They come from a wide array of people, some of whom you may have heard of and some perhaps you won't. They are here for you to use as a daily fix. You won't always have the time to reread the whole book but this section can be reviewed very quickly and may serve to inspire when you need to know you are not alone in messing things up. Making mistakes is a human condition and one we all share. No one, however, as easy as they make it seem, gets it right all the time. The most courageous share their thoughts. I've even included some blank space for you to add your own should you be so inclined. This is a work-in-progress so to speak.

Bear in mind, such quotes are designed to motivate immediately. Often just reading a few of them is enough to plant a seed or two of thought-provoking reflection and help change your attitude. Their lasting appeal is their ability to comfort and motivate when needed. In that spirit, I have provided you with 196 of the most meaningful maxims on mistakes and failures, which will provide you with **an aphorism a day** for 6 months (with a few spare ones for good measure).

Business Leaders and Business Thinkers

"Do not be embarrassed by your failures, learn from them and start again." **Richard Branson, British Founder and CEO, Virgin Group**

"If you don't make mistakes, you can't make decisions." **Warren Buffett, American Chairman and CEO, Berkshire Hathaway**

"Failure doesn't have to be an F-word. Take these setbacks in stride; remember that a goal that can be achieved in a single step is probably not even meaningful or ambitious." **Reid Hoffman, American Founder of LinkedIn**

"If something is important enough, you should try even if the probable outcome is failure." **Elon Musk, South African Founder of Tesla Motors and Space X and co-Founder of PayPal**

"Even if you fail at your ambitious thing, it's very hard to fail completely. That's the thing that people don't get." **Larry Page, American co-Founder of Google**

"First, some of the most important and insightful learning is far more likely to come from failures than from successes. Second, the learning has to be institutionalized to endure. Otherwise you keep making the same mistakes over and over, and you don't learn from them. The topic of failure is very important, and it gets more lip service than good practice. I think I learned more from my failures than from my successes in all my years as a CEO, I think of my failures as a gift." **A.G. Lafley, American CEO of Procter & Gamble**

"Embracing failure is as important as toasting success." **Linda Rottenberg, American Lawyer and Businesswoman**

"The difference between a crisis and an opportunity is WHEN you learn about it." **Alan Webber, American Businessman and Author**

"Fail often in order to succeed sooner." **IDEO's slogan**

Failure usually comes early; successes take time. **Venture Capitalists' mantra**

"Anything can look like a failure in the middle." **Rosabeth Moss Kanter, American Professor at Harvard Business School**

"I've learned that mistakes can often be as good a teacher as success." **Jack Welch, American CEO of General Electric**

"Reward worthy failure – Experimentation." **Bill Gates, American CEO of Microsoft**

"How you deal with failure determines part of your success as a leader." **Kim Clark, former Dean, Harvard Business School**

"The only way that I've learned anything is through failure." **Martin Cooper, American Inventor of the cellphone**

"It's not what we do well that enables us to achieve in the long run. It's what we do wrong and how we correct it that ensures ... our long lasting success." **Bernie Marcus, American co-Founder of Home Depot**

"You don't learn to walk by following rules. You learn by doing, and by falling over." **Richard Branson, British Founder and CEO, Virgin Group**

"You want to learn from experience, but you want to learn from other people's experience when you can." **Warren Buffett, American Chairman and CEO, Berkshire Hathaway**

"Failure is just part of the process of getting to world-class. Screw-ups are the mark of excellence." **Tom Peters, American Writer on Business Management practices**

"Failure is not a single, cataclysmic event. You don't fail overnight. Instead, failure is a few errors in judgment, repeated every day." **Jim Rohn, American Business thinker**

"Nothing fails like success." **Robert Carrion, CEO and Chairman of Banco Popular De Puerto Rico**

"Would you like me to give you a formula for... success? It's quite simple, really. Double your rate of failure. You're thinking of failure as the enemy of success. But it isn't at all... you can be discouraged by failure or you can learn from it. So go ahead and make mistakes. Make all you can. Because that's where you'll find success. On the far side." **Thomas Watson, American Founder of IBM**

"With engineering, I view this year's failure as next year's opportunity to try it again. Failures are not something to be avoided. You want to have them happen as quickly as you can so you can make progress rapidly." **Gordon Moore, American Technologist and Author of Moore's Law**

"Sometimes when you innovate, you make mistakes. It is best to admit them quickly, and get on with improving your other innovations." **Steve Jobs, American former CEO of Apple**

"I've learned that mistakes can often be as good a teacher as success." Jack Welch, **American former CEO of General Electric**

"Success builds character, failure reveals it." **Dave Checketts, American Businessman**

"Real leaders always stop to learn from their mistakes." **Alan Webber, American Author and former Editor of Harvard Business Review**

"Failure teaches lessons that can't be learned any other way." **Alan Webber, American Author and former Editor of Harvard Business Review**

"It turns out that the factor that explains their success at the beginning is what accounts for their failure later." **John Doerr, American Venture Capitalist**

"Learn from your mistakes. It's all right to get your fingers crushed in the door, but don't let the same door crush them twice." **T. Boone Pickens, American Financier**

"Failure is success if we learn from it." **Malcolm Forbes, American former Publisher of Forbes Magazine**

"As we go through life, we are taught lessons which we may or may not choose to learn." **Herminia Ibarra, Cuban Professor at INSEAD Business School**

"Wall Street people learn nothing and forget everything." **Benjamin Graham, British-born American professional Investor**

"Oh, I'm sure I've made my share of mistakes. I don't think I've made more than my fair share of them, although I think more has been made of the ones that I've made." **Carly Fiorina, American former CEO of Hewlett-Packard**

"One way to succeed is to work hard at not failing by always anticipating problems before they occur." **Peter Drucker, Austrian-American Business Management Thinker**

"Who's the worst boss you ever had? Don't be like him. Who's the best boss you ever had. Be like him!" **Dee Hock, American Founder of VISA**

"I have found that I always learn more from my mistakes than from my successes. If you aren't making some mistakes, you aren't taking enough chances." **John Sculley, American former CEO of Apple Computer**

"Don't be afraid to make a mistake. But make sure you don't make the same mistake twice." **Akio Morita, Japanese Founder and former CEO of Sony Electronics**

"Success is 99% failure." **Soichiro Honda, Japanese Founder and CEO of Honda Motor Company**

"Always make new mistakes." **Esther Dyson, American Author and Technology Commentator**

"Failure is the opportunity to begin again more intelligently." **Henry Ford, American industrialist and founder and CEO of Ford Motor Company**

"Do the one thing you think you cannot do. Fail at it. Try again. Do better the second time. The only people who never tumble are those who never mount the high wire. This is your moment. Own it." **Oprah Winfrey, American businesswoman and Talk Show Host**

"We used to write this down by saying, 'move fast and break things.' And the idea was, unless you are breaking some stuff you are not moving fast enough. I think there's probably something in that for other entrepreneurs to learn which is that making mistakes is okay. At the end of the day, the goal of building something is to build something, not to not make mistakes." **Mark Zuckerberg, American Founder and CEO of Facebook**

"Don't be afraid to fail. You can't experiment without failure. And you can't compete if you don't try. The best thing about technology today is that it allows you to do things quickly — and often with minimal investment — to sample them. To keep up and succeed today, you need to adopt a "rinse-wash-and-repeat" mentality." **Alex Campbell, American co-founder and chief innovation officer of Vibes**

"What we learn from history is that people don't learn from history." **Warren Buffett, American Chairman and CEO, Berkshire Hathaway**

"[My biggest mistake is probably] weighing too much on someone's talent and not someone's personality. I think it matters whether someone has a good heart." **Elon Musk, South African Founder of Tesla Motors and Space X and co-founder of PayPal**

"But one of the big things we do at Google is we try and launch early and iterate and learn from both our successes and our failures." **Marissa Mayer, American former Vice-President at Google and currently CEO of Yahoo**

Presidents, Prime Ministers, Political and Military Leaders

"Never interrupt your enemy when he is making a mistake." **Napoleon Bonaparte, General and first President of France**

"Failure is an orphan, but victory has a thousand fathers." **John F. Kennedy, 35th U.S. President**

"Success is going from failure to failure without losing enthusiasm." **Winston Churchill, former British Prime Minister**

"Only those who dare to fail greatly can ever achieve greatly." **Robert F. Kennedy, American former U.S. Attorney General**

"We ought not to look back, unless it is to derive useful lessons from past errors and for the purpose of profiting by dear bought experience." **George Washington, American General and first U.S. President**

"The ultimate measure of a man is not where he stands in moments of comfort and convenience, but where he stands at times of challenge." **Martin Luther King, Jr., American Civil Rights Leader**

"Confession of errors is like a broom which sweeps away the dirt and leaves the surface brighter and clearer. I feel stronger for confession." **Mahatma Gandhi, Indian Political Leader and former Prime Minister**

"It is hard to fail, but it is worse never to have tried to succeed." **Theodore "Teddy" Roosevelt, 26th U.S. President**

"Success contains within it the germs of failure, and the reverse is also true." **Charles de Gaulle, French General and former President of France**

"The worst mistake is to have the best ladder and the wrong wall." **Donald Rumsfeld, American Politician and former U.S. Secretary of Defense**

"It's worse than a crime, it's a mistake." **Charles Talleyrand, French Revolutionary and Diplomat**

"All men make mistakes, but only wise men learn from their mistakes." **Winston Churchill, former British Prime Minister**

"A good friend who points out mistakes and imperfections and rebukes evil is to be respected as if he reveals a secret of hidden treasure." **Buddha, Nepalese-Indian Spiritual Leader and Teacher**

"My guess is that people tend not to fall in exactly the same potholes that their predecessors do. More often than not, they make original mistakes. We all do." **Donald Rumsfeld, American Politician and former U.S. Secretary of Defense**

"No man ever became great or good except through many and great mistakes." **William Gladstone, former British Prime Minister**

"There are no secrets to success. It is the result of preparation, hard work, and learning from failure." **Colin Powell, American General and former U.S. Secretary of State**

"Freedom is not worth having if it does not include the freedom to make mistakes." **Mahatma K. Gandhi, Indian Political Leader and former Prime Minister**

"The greatest general is he who makes the fewest mistakes." **Napoleon Bonaparte, French General and first President of France**

"I also had one more mistake to add to my lifelong résumé of mistakes, the curriculum vitae for all wisdom and knowledge." Pete Blaber, **U.S. Army Delta Force Commander**

"So I made a mistake. That happens. It proves I'm human." **Hillary Rodham Clinton, American former First Lady and 67ᵗʰ U.S. Secretary of State**

"I learned that good judgment comes from experience and that experience grows out of mistakes." **Omar Bradley, former U.S. Army General**

"I have so often in my life been mistaken that I no longer blush for it." **Napoleon Bonaparte, French General and first President of France**

"You like to respect and admire someone whom you love, but actually, you love even more the people who require understanding and who make mistakes and have to grow with their mistakes." **Eleanor Roosevelt, American former U.S. First Lady**

"It can be helpful to study the experiences of competitors to see how they have handled, or failed to handle, various crises. One would have thought, for example, that the officials at BP would have studied the mistakes made during the Exxon Valdez oil spill in order to handle a similar situation mores skillfully ... Mistakes will always be made, but the least we can do is try to make original mistakes, rather than repeating old ones." **Donald Rumsfeld, American Politician and former U.S. Secretary of Defense**

"An error does not become a truth by reason of multiplied propagation, nor does truth become error because nobody sees it." **Mahatma K. Gandhi, Indian Political Leader and former Prime Minister**

"If you live long enough, you'll make mistakes. But if you learn from them, you'll be a better person. It's how you handle adversity, not how it affects you. The main thing is never quit, never quit, never quit." **Bill Clinton, 42ⁿᵈ U.S. President**

Historians, Philosophers and Proverbs

"To make no mistakes is not in the power of man; but from their errors and mistakes the wise and good learn wisdom for the future." **Plutarch, Greek Historian**

"Do not be embarrassed by your mistakes. Nothing can teach us better than our understanding of them. This is one of the best ways of self-education." **Thomas Carlyle, Scottish Philosopher, Satirical Writer, Essayist, Historian and Teacher**

"A stumble may prevent a fall." **Thomas Fuller, English Historian**

"Leaders learn from their mistakes. To succeed, leaders must acknowledge and understand and improve on their shortcomings." **Doris Kearns Goodwin, American Historian**

"While the improvident derive injury even from their successes, characters of the opposite stamp actually find a road to improvement through their set-backs." **Polybius, Greek Historian**

"Persistent people begin their success where others end in failure." **Edward Eggleston, American Historian and Novelist**

"If one has made a mistake, and fails to correct it, one has made a greater mistake." **Plato, Greek Philosopher**

"A great nation is like a great man; when he makes a mistake, he realizes it. Having realized it, he admits it. Having admitted it, he corrects it. He considers those who point out his faults as his most benevolent teachers." **Lao Tzu, Chinese Philosopher**

"All courses of action are risky, so prudence is not in avoiding danger but calculating risk and acting decisively. Make mistakes of ambition and not mistakes of sloth. Develop the strength to do bold things, not the strength to suffer." **Niccolò Machiavelli, Italian Philosopher and Author**

"The first step towards amendment is the recognition of error." **Seneca, Roman Philosopher**

"The greatest of faults is to be conscious of none." **Thomas Carlyle, Scottish Philosopher, Writer, Historian and Teacher**

"From the errors of others, a wise man corrects his own." **Publilius Syrus, Syrian Writer of Maxims**

"A man who has committed a mistake and doesn't correct it is committing another mistake." **Confucius, Chinese Philosopher**

"Learn to distinguish the difference between errors of knowledge and breaches of morality." **Ayn Rand, American Novelist and Philosopher**

"Pay attention to your enemies, for they are the first to discover your mistakes." **Antisthenes, Greek Philosopher**

"Never waste the opportunities offered by a good crisis." **Niccolò Machiavelli, Italian Philosopher and Author**

"The great virtue of man lies in his ability to correct his mistakes and to continually make a new man of himself." **Wang Yang-Ming, Chinese Philosopher**

"Any man can make mistakes, but only an idiot persists in his error." **Cicero, Roman Philosopher and Politician**

"Those who cannot remember the past are condemned to repeat it." **George Santayana, Spanish Philosopher**

"We learn little from our successes, but a lot from our failures." **Arab Proverb**

"Be not ashamed of mistakes and thus make them crimes." **Confucian Proverb**

"Fall seven times and stand up eight." **Japanese Proverb**

"That which we obtain too easily, we esteem too lightly."
Unknown origin

"Wise men learn by other men's mistakes, fools by the their own." **Unknown origin**

Sports Figures

"The person who is afraid to risk failure seldom has to face success. I expected my players to make mistakes, as long as they were mistakes of commission. A mistake of commission happens when you are doing what should be done but don't get the results you want." **John Wooden, American College Basketball Coach**

"Football is a game of errors. The team that makes the fewest errors in a game usually wins." **Paul Brown, American Football Coach and Owner**

"The mistakes are all there waiting to be made." **Savielly Tartakower, Polish and French chess master**

"Every strike brings me closer to the next home run." **Babe Ruth, American Baseball player**

"Failure is not fatal, but failure to change might be." **John Wooden, American Basketball Coach**

"One learns from defeat, not from victory." **Bobby Jones, American Golfer**

"Failure is good. It's fertilizer. Everything I've learned about coaching, I've learned from making mistakes." **Rick Pitino, American Basketball Coach**

"Coaching is nothing more than eliminating mistakes before you get fired." **Lou Holtz, American College Football Coach**

"I've failed over and over and over again in my life and that is why I succeed." **Michael Jordan, American Basketball Player**

"Mistakes are made. But, fundamentally, if you're sound, you eliminate as many mistakes as possible." **Wayne Gretzky, Canadian Hockey Player**

"Most ball games are lost, not won." **Casey Stengel, American Baseball Player and Manager**

Poets, Playwrights and Novelists

"Men succeed when they realize that their failures are the preparation for their victories." **Ralph Waldo Emerson, American Poet**
"Mistakes are their own instructors." **Horace, Roman Poet**
"Try again. Fail again. Fail better." **Samuel Beckett, Irish Novelist and Playwright**
"A life spent making mistakes is not only more honorable, but more useful than a life spent doing nothing." **George Bernard Shaw, Irish Playwright**
"Experience is simply the name we give to our mistakes." **Oscar Wilde, Irish Writer and Poet**
"It is impossible to live without failing at something, unless you live so cautiously that you might as well not have lived at all." **J.K. Rowling, British Novelist**
"It is better to be young in your failures than old in your successes." **Flannery O'Connor, American Novelist**
"A man of genius makes no mistakes. His errors ... are the portals to discovery." **James Joyce, Irish Author and Playwright**
"If I had my life to live over... I'd dare to make more mistakes next time." **Nadine Stair, American Poet**
"A subtle thought that is in error may yet give rise to fruitful inquiry that can establish truths of great value." **Isaac Asimov, Science Fiction and Popular Science Book Writer**
"Success does not consist in never making mistakes but in never making the same one a second time." **George Bernard Shaw, Irish Playwright**
"Our praise is not measured in our in abilities not to fall whether in our abilities to stand up after the fall." **Walt Whitman, American Poet**

"Sometimes we may learn more from a man's errors, than from his virtues." **Henry Longfellow, American Poet**

"There are many victories worse than defeat." **George Eliot, English Novelist**

"If we could be twice young and twice old, we could correct all our mistakes." **Euripides, Greek Playwright**

"Everything popular is wrong." **Oscar Wilde, Irish Writer and Poet**

"There are no mistakes in life, there are only lessons to be learned: advice to the youth." **Mark Twain, American Novelist**

"Good people are good because they've come to wisdom through failure." **William Saroyan, American Dramatist and Author**

"Failure is the condiment that gives success its flavor." **Truman Capote, American Author and Playwright**

"Man approaches the unattainable truth through a succession of errors." **Aldous Huxley, English Novelist**

"Often the difference between a successful person and a failure is not one has better abilities or ideas, but the courage that one has to bet on one's ideas, to take a calculated risk — and to act." **Andre Malraux, French Novelist**

"Errors like straws upon the surface flow: Who would search for pearls must dive below." **John Dryden, English Poet**

"History doesn't repeat itself, but sometimes it rhymes." **Mark Twain, American Novelist**

"Science, my lad, is made up of mistakes, but they are mistakes which it is useful to make, because they lead little by little to the truth." **Jules Verne, French Science Fiction Writer**

"Success and failure are both difficult to endure. Along with success come drugs, divorce, fornication, bullying, travel, meditation, medication, depression, neurosis and suicide. With failure comes failure." **Joseph Heller, American Novelist**

"If only we could have two lives: the first in which to make one's mistakes, which seem as if they have to be made; and the second in which to profit by them." **D.H. Lawrence, English Novelist**

Inventors, Scientists, Economists and Doctors

"I have not failed, I've just found ten thousand ways that won't work." **Thomas Edison, American Inventor**

"Failure is an option here. If things are not failing, you are not innovating enough." **Elon Musk, South African Inventor of the Tesla Electric Car**

"How few there are who have courage enough to own their faults, or resolution enough to mend them." **Ben Franklin, American Inventor**

"To kill an error is as good a service as, and sometimes even better than, the establishing of a new truth or fact." **Charles Darwin, English Naturalist**

"An expert is a person who has made all of the mistakes that can be made in a very narrow field." **Niels Bohr, Danish Physicist and 1922 Nobel Prize winner in Physics**

"Do not be afraid of making mistakes, for there is no other way of learning how to live!" **Alfred Adler, Austrian Doctor and Psychotherapist**

"If you don't make mistakes, you're not working on hard enough problems. And that's a big mistake." **Frank Wilczek, American Theoretical Physicist and 2004 Nobel Prize winner in Physics**

"The only mistake in life is the lesson not learned." **Albert Einstein, German-born Theoretical Physicist**

"If all else fails, immortality can always be assured by spectacular error." **John Kenneth Galbraith, Canadian-American Economist**

"From error to error, one discovers the entire truth." **Sigmund Freud, Austrian Neurologist and Founding Father of Psychoanalysis**

"The most valuable thing you can make is a mistake — you can't learn anything from being perfect." **Adam Osborne, British-American Computer Designer**

"An error doesn't become a mistake until you refuse to correct it." **O.A. Battista, Canadian-American Chemist and Author**

"It is the true nature of mankind to learn from mistakes, not from example." **Fred Hoyle, English Astronomer**

"You want to be extra rigorous about making the best possible thing you can. Find everything that's wrong with it and fix it. Seek negative feedback, particularly from friends." **Elon Musk, South African Inventor of the Tesla Electric Car and Founder of SpaceX**

"The definition of insanity is doing the same thing over and over again and expecting different results." **Albert Einstein, German-born Theoretical Physicist**

Actors, Artists, Painters, Sculptors, Composers & Musicians

"Mistakes are part of the dues one pays for a full life." **Sophia Loren, Italian Actress**

"If I had to live my life again, I'd make the same mistakes, only sooner." **Tallulah Bankhead, American Actress**

"Mistakes are almost always of a sacred nature. Never try to correct them. On the contrary: rationalize them, understand them thoroughly. After that, it will be possible for you to sublimate them." **Salvador Dali, Spanish-Catalan Artist and Surrealist Movement Leader**

"Mishaps are like knives, that either serve us or cut us, as we grasp them by the blade or by the handle." **James Russell Lowell, American Poet**

"If you have made mistakes, even serious ones, there is always another chance for you. What we call failure is not the falling down, but the staying down." **Mary Pickford, Canadian-American Actress, co-founder of United Artists and of the Academy of Motion Picture Arts and Sciences**

"I honestly think it is better to be a failure at something you love than to be a success at something you hate." **George Burns, American Comedian**

"The greatest danger for most of us is not our aim is too high and we miss it, but that it is too low and we reach it." **Michelangelo, Italian Sculptor, Painter and Architect**

"I have learned throughout my life as a composer chiefly through my mistakes and pursuits of false assumptions, not by my exposure to founts of wisdom and knowledge." **Igor Stravinsky, Russian Composer and Pianist**

"In order to succeed, your desire for success should be greater than your fear of failure." **Bill Cosby, American Comedian and Actor**

"My life has been nothing but a failure, and all that's left for me is to destroy my paintings before I disappear." **Claude Monet, French Painter**

"We can afford almost any mistake once." **Joe E. Lewis, American Comedian and Singer**

"Even the knowledge of my own infallibility cannot keep me from making mistakes. Only when I fall do I get up again." **Vincent Van Gogh, Dutch Painter**

"Eighty percent of success is showing up." **Woody Allen, American Actor, Screenwriter and Film Director**

"Creativity is allowing yourself to make mistakes. Art is knowing which ones to keep." **Scott Adams, American Cartoonist and creator of "Dilbert"**

"The only real mistake is the one from which we learn nothing." **John Powell, American Composer**

"You're my favorite mistake." **Sheryl Crow, American Singer and Songwriter**

"I've been imitated so well I've heard people copy my mistakes." **Jimi Hendrix, American Guitarist**

"I have a theory that the only original things we ever do are mistakes." **Billy Joel, American Singer and Songwriter**

"In order to succeed, your desire for success should be greater than your fear of failure." **Bill Cosby, American Comedian and Actor**

Non-Fiction Authors, Scholars and Teachers

"Failure truly is essential to success ... Failure is a gift. Failure has been so helpful to me. It's taken me closer to my dreams, equipped me with more knowledge and toughened me up so I'm more prepared. Success and failure go hand in hand. They are business partners." **Robin Sharma, Canadian Lawyer, Leadership Expert and Writer**

"A failure is a man who has blundered, but is not able to cash in on the experience." **Elbert Hubbard, American Writer and Philosopher**

"For the robust, an error is information; for the fragile, an error is an error." **Nassim Nicholas Taleb, Lebanese American Essayist and Scholar**

"It is a mistake to suppose that men succeed through success; they much oftener succeed through failures." **Samuel Smiles, Scottish Author**

"The potential for success is around every corner, but you cannot have it until you fail." **Colin Rich, American Photographer and Cinematographer**

"We have forty-million reasons for failure — but not a single excuse." **Rudyard Kipling, British Author**

"One of the reasons mature people stop learning is that they become less and less willing to risk failure." **John W. Gardner, American Author**

"Failure is the tuition you pay for success." **Walter Brunell, American Author**

"Just as philosophy is the study of other people's misconceptions, so history is the study of other people's mistakes." **Philip Guedala, British Lawyer and Writer**

"Mistakes are a fact of life. It is the response to error that counts." **Nikki Giovanni, American Author, Activist, Commentator and Educator**

"Most great people have attained their greatest success just one step beyond their greatest failure." **Napoleon Hill, American Author**

"The beauty of 'spacing' children many years apart lies in the fact that parents have time to learn the mistakes that were made with the older ones — which permits them to make exactly the opposite mistakes with the younger ones." **Sydney J. Harris, American Journalist**

"A second-class effort is a first-class mistake." **William Arthur Ward, American Author**

"Failure is simply a few errors in judgment, repeated every day." **Jim Rohn, American self-help Author**

"We learn wisdom from failure much more than from success. We often discover what will do, by finding out what will not do; and probably he who never made a mistake never made a discovery." **Samuel Smiles, Scottish Author**

"Remember the two benefits of failure. First, if you do fail, you learn what doesn't work; and second, the failure gives you the opportunity to try a new approach." **Roger Von Oech, American Author**

"Failure is the path of least persistence." **Michael Larsen, American Literary Agent**

"There are defeats more triumphant than victories." **Michel de Montaigne, French Essayist**

"A mistake is only a mistake if you make it twice." **Robin Sharma, Canadian Lawyer, Leadership Expert and Writer**

"The successful man will profit from his mistakes and try again in a different way." **Dale Carnegie, American self-help Author**

"The only person who never makes mistakes is the person who never does anything." Denis Waitley, **American Motivational Speaker and Writer**

"The weak shows his strength and hides his weaknesses; the magnificent exhibits his weaknesses like ornaments." **Nassim Nicholas Taleb, Lebanese American Essayist and Scholar**

"An intelligent person is never afraid or ashamed to find errors in his understanding of things." Bryant H. McGill, **American Author, Speaker and Self-development and Human Rights Activist**

JOIN THE MAGNIFICENT MISTAKE COMMUNITY

Would you like to join a global community of people who share their mistakes, but also the valuable lessons they took from them? For more information, please visit:

www.IonValis.com/the-magnificent-mistake.html

You can sign up to our exclusive newsletter there. **Never miss out on new tutorials, tips and updates and get access to free, color PDF templates of the** *Magnificent Mistake*[TM] *Workbook,* including:

- **3 examples of** *Mistake Maps*[TM]
- **a sample** *Mistake Journal*[TM] **page**
- **an example of the M.A.S.T.E.R. Checklist**[TM] **in action.**

Note From the Author: Reviews are gold to authors. If you've enjoyed this book, would you consider rating it and reviewing it on www.Amazon.com or www.Goodreads.com?

ACKNOWLEDGEMENTS

I have often likened the writing of a book to climbing Mount Everest. (For the record, I have only recently achieved the former but have my moments when I aspire to accomplish the latter.) To my mind, there are a lot of similarities between completing your magnum opus and summiting a Himalayan peak. First, both are challenging tests of determination, will and skill. Second, they equally require lots of help from others — sherpas and guides on the mountain face, and friends and family when facing either the blank page or the overly worded one.

I am incredibly grateful to the many friends who inspired, encouraged and occasionally indulged me in this long trek. My former colleague Steve Hardy lit the spark in me for both blogging and business book writing, and I might not have even considered turning an initial essay on "The Magnificent Mistake" into this book without his enthusiastic prompting. A number of great friends – David Danon, Adrian Letts, Germaine Gibara, Szandra Szilvassy, Farlan Dowell, Iain Henderson, Mike Ross, Ben Grass, Matt Finkelstein, Sascha Eiblmayr, Megan Latta, Brad Smith, and Lynn Latta – extended to me the extreme generosity of their time and intellect in reading early (and far too rough) drafts of this manuscript. Andy Nulman and Jon Kay gave me lots of great advice on the book business in general, and the business of writing a book in particular.

As well, I was blessed to have an incredibly supportive family to encourage me in this endeavor. I spent a glorious fortnight a few summers ago in what seemed like a graduate seminar on error, discussing and debating some of the ideas in this book with two of the best minds I know — my father Kimon and my late uncle-from-another-family W. Lambert (Scotty) Gardiner. My brother Paris was also a source of encouragement, and I return the favor now by urging him to complete his screenplay.

In the final stages of this long process, I was often guided, occasionally cajoled, and from time to time admonished by my peerless editor Wanda Potrykus. In every instance, however, the manuscript improved as a result — and for that I am extremely grateful.

As John F. Kennedy famously observed: "victory has a thousand fathers but defeat is an orphan." To paraphrase him, I have all these people and many more to thank if we've succeeded in making this is a meaningful work; however, any errors or shortcomings are mine alone.

NOTES

AUTHOR'S NOTE

[1] I first came up with the expression "magnificent mistake" in 2007, when I wrote an essay on why we should study failures rather than successes for my blog, *Pop Philosophy*. Later, after researching and writing this book, I discovered that I was not the first to be entranced by this wonderful, alliterative phrase. Nineteenth Century American writer Henry James used it for the first time in his novel, *The Next Time*. In it, he introduced the world to other, similar collocations such as "hideous triumph" and "exquisite failure." James became quite fond of the "magnificent mistake" expression, and used it again in his non-fiction book, *English Hours: A Portrait of a Country:*

"For it was a city, the main port of Suffolk, as even its poor relics show; with a fleet of its own on the North Sea, and a big religious house on the hill. We wonder what were then the apparent conditions of security, and on what rough calculation a community could so build itself to meet its fate. It keeps one easy company here today to think of the whole business as a *magnificent mistake* (italics added for emphasis)."

James shared my fascination with mistakes, it seems. His first short story was entitled "A Tragedy of Error" which he published at the tender age of 21.

Preface

[1] Stanford Graduate School of Business Case Study, "Southwest Airlines (A)" by Charles A. O'Reilly and Jeffrey Pfeffer, 27 pages. Publication Date: Jan. 01, 1995. Prod. # HR1A-PDF-ENG

[2] Timothy Ferriss, *The Four Hour Work Week: Escape 9-5, Live Anywhere, And Join the New Rich* (New York, Crown Publishers, 2007), page 34

[3] To get a full appreciation for the impact of Peter Drucker's magnum opus, *The Effective Executive* (New York: Harper Business, 1993), read it. It's still as relevant today as it was when it was first written in 1965. Incidentally, I was recommended to read this book by none other than then-Speaker of the House of Representatives Newt Gingrich. In 1994, he urged every staff member working on Capitol Hill to read that book in order to know learn how to be effective.

Introduction

[1] *Sports Illustrated*, August 25, 2008. To see the photo finish, go to: http://beijing2008.blogs.nytimes.com/2008/08/16/the-phelps-cavic-photo-finish/?_php=true&_type=blogs&_r=0

[2] Ibid., *Sports Illustrated*

[3] Senator Mitch McConnell (R-KY) introduced me to this Southern saying. He was quoted in the October 18, 2013 article on NBC News.com entitled "Congress: McConnell: 'No Need

for a Second Mule Kick' http://www.nbcnews.com/news/other/congress-mcconnell-no-need-second-mule-kick-f8C11417530

CHAPTER 1: WHY

[1] For more information on how the Brain Port works, see http://discovermagazine.com/2008/jul/23-the-blind-climber-who-sees-through-his-tongue#.UUI-cqVe_1E

[2] I first learned about the three epic attempts by George Mallory to conquer Mount Everest in the excellent 2010 documentary, *The Wildest Dream: Conquest of Everest,* directed by Anthony Geffen

[3] David Eagleman, *Incognito: The Secret Lives of the Brain,* (New York: Vintage Books, 2011) pages 40-41

[4] Malcolm Gladwell, *Outliers: The Story of Success* (New York: Little, Brown and Company, 2008), pages 48-50

[5] For an interesting dissection of the companies profiled by *In Search of Excellence* by Tom Peters and Robert Waterman, see this article in *Forbes Magazine:* http://www.forbes.com/2002/10/04/1004excellent.html

[6] Rudyard Kipling, "If". To read (and listen to) this amazing poem, go to: http://www.poemhunter.com/poem/if/

[7] David Maraniss, *First In His Class: A Biography of Bill Clinton* (New York: Simon & Schuster, 1995), pages 384-389

[8] David Remnick is quoted from the following National Public Radio article: http://www.npr.org/templates/story/story.php?storyId=125595945&ps=rs

[9] J.K. Rowling Speaks at 2008 Harvard University Commencement Address: http://vimeo.com/1711302

[10] For the iconic Nike ad where Michael Jordan talks about his failures, see: https://www.youtube.com/watch?v=45mMioJ5szc

[11] Wikipedia entry on Ted Williams: http://en.wikipedia.org/wiki/Ted_Williams

[12] Daniel Coyle, *The Talent Code: Greatness Isn't Born. It's Grown. Here's How,* (New York: Bantam Books, 2009), pages 4-5

CHAPTER 2: WHO

[1] Buffett calls Dexter Shoe his worst deal ever' – Reuters, February 29, 2008

[2] Mary Buffett and David Clark, *The Tao of Warren Buffett* (London: Simon & Schuster UK, 2008) page 117

[3] Ibid., *The Tao of Warren Buffett,* page 54

[4] I learned about the CoE from an in-depth interview on April 4, 2010 with a former Amazon employee who asked to be questioned on background. He generously shared the information on the CoE – current at the time of the interview — from the

internal Amazon Wiki, and I have reproduced it in its entirety here. In a second interview with a separate and still current Amazon employee (who also wanted to stay off the record) on April 14, 2013, I confirmed the continued use of the CoE at Amazon today. Curiously, the second employee refused to confirm that the CoE stood for "Collection of Errors" even though I asked him repeatedly if that was the case. Amazon has a well-developed reputation for secrecy surrounding its internal processes, and this employee's behavior seemed consistent with that view.

[5] Much of the background on Amazon's growth is sourced from the book by Richard L. Brandt, *One Click: Jeff Bezos and the Rise of Amazon.com* (New York: Portfolio/Penguin, 2012)

[6] Ajaz Ahmed and Stefan Olander, *Velocity: The Seven New Laws For a World Gone Digital,* London: Vermilion, 2012, page 10

[7] Ibid., *One Click*

[8] I leaned heavily on David Magee's magisterial book on Toyota - *How Toyota Became #1: Leadership Lessons from the World's Greatest Car Company* (New York: Portfolio/Penguin, 2007) — for the section on the Japanese automaker.

[9] *Be, Know, Do: Leadership the Army Way (Adapted from the Official Army Leadership Manual),* (San Francisco: Leader to Leader Institute, 2004), pages 136-151

[10] Ibid., *Be, Know, Do*

[11] For more information on AARs, see: http://www.au.af.mil/au/awc/awcgate/army/tc_25-20/tc25-20.pdf

[12] Ibid., *Be, Know, Do*

[13] For more information on CALL, see: http://usacac.army.mil/cac2/call/index.asp

[14] For the biographical information on former General David Petraeus, I relied on the book by David Cloud and Greg Jaffe, *The Fourth Star: Four Generals and the Epic Struggle for the Future of the United States Army* (New York: Crown Publishers, 2009)

[15] Pete Blaber, *The Men, The Mission and Me: Lessons from a Former Delta Operator* (New York, Berkley Caliber, 2008)

[16] Eric Haney, *Inside Delta Force: The Story of America's Elite Counterterrorist Unit,* (New York, Bantam Dell, 2005), pages 174-177

[17] I am indebted to Major Amnon Shefler, who sat with me for a long interview on January 27, 2010 to tell me about his experiences in the Israeli Air Force, and in particular how the IAF dealt with failure and mistakes. The information in this case study comes in large measure from the direct experience of Major Shefler.

[18] Garry Kasparov, *How Life Imitates Chess: Making the Right Moves, From the Board to the Board Room,* (New York: Bloomsbury USA, 2007), pages 144-145

[19] The late Ayrton Senna's thoughts on error are quoted from interviews from the excellent 2010 documentary *Senna*, directed by Asif Kapadia.

CHAPTER 3: HOW

[1] "Learning from the Bay of Pigs Disaster", NPR.org, April 17, 2011: http://www.npr.org/2011/04/17/135444482/50-years-later-learning-from-the-bay-of-pigs

[2] Jim Rasenberger, *The Brilliant Disaster: JFK, Castro, and America's Doomed Invasion of Cuba's Bay of Pigs*

[3] *Harvard Business Review*, Interview with A.G. Lafley, "I Think of My Failures as a Gift", April 2011

[4] Chip Heath and Dan Heath, *Decisive: How to Make Better Choices in Life and Work* (Toronto: Random House Canada, 2013), pages 130-131

[5] Atul Gewande, *The Checklist Manifesto: How To Get Things Right*

[6] Ibid., Garry Kasparov, *How Life Imitates Chess*

[7] Thomas Barnett, *The Pentagon's New Map: War and Peace in the Twenty-First Century*, (New York: Berkley Books, 2004) page 115

[8] For more information on Barbara Tuchman's masterpiece, *The Guns of August*, see: http://www.amazon.com/The-Guns-August-Pulitzer-Prize-Winning/dp/0345476093

CHAPTER 4: NOW

[1] *Men's Health,* June 2014, "Turn Your Idea Into $57 Million" by Eric Spitznagel

[2] For more information on The Marine Corps' 70% Solution, see this video: https://www.youtube.com/watch?v=sWolwQ0MgOg

[3] *Fast Company,* April 2014, "Pixar's Motto: Going from Suck to Non-Suck", http://www.fastcompany.com/1742431/pixars-motto-going-suck-nonsuck

[4] "If" by Rudyard Kipling

[5] *Harvard Business Review,* "How to Avoid Catastrophe" by Catherine H. Tinsley, Robin L. Dillon, and Peter M. Madsen, April 2011

[6] Ibid., "How to Avoid Catastrophe"

[7] Ibid., "Pixar's Motto: Going from Suck to Non-Suck"

[8] Duke University professor of management Sim Sitkin's concept of "intelligent failures" is discussed in *Harvard Business Review,* "Strategies For Learning From Failure" by Amy C. Edmondson

[9] *Harvard Business Review,* "Why Leaders Don't Learn from Success" by Francesca Gino and Gary P. Pisano, April 2011

[10] For more information on Engineers without Borders Failure Reports, see "Confession is Good for the Corporate Soul" by Bob Ramsay, *The Globe and Mail*, July 25, 2012: http://www.theglobeandmail.com/globe-debate/confessions-good-for-the-corporate-soul/article4438831/

[11] Richard Guha, http://mengonline.com/blog/2013/03/20/why-id-rather-hire-someone-who-has-failed-twice-than-some-on-who-has-succeeded-once-by-richard-guha-3/

ABOUT THE AUTHOR

Ion is a strategic advisor to individuals and organizations, where he helps both employees and executives accelerate their development, reinvent themselves periodically and transform their errors into magnificent mistakes.

He has a unique combination of entrepreneurial and executive experience in both the public and private sectors. Ion has worked as a Press Secretary on Capitol Hill in Washington, DC, helped launch and run a ground-breaking international mobile media initiative at the world's largest mobile phone company in London, served as a senior executive in a fast-growing technology start-up in Montreal, and for the past 6 years has run a strategic advice firm with clients in North America and Europe.

Ion consults, speaks and writes about leadership, professional development and organizational reinvention at www. IonValis.com and also provides social commentary on his blog Pop Philosophy.

www.ingramcontent.com/pod-product-compliance
Lightning Source LLC
Chambersburg PA
CBHW021925190326
41519CB00009B/913